Quick Meals

Great fast meals for family and friends

THE AUSTRALIAN
Women's Weekly

NZ, Canada, US and UK readers
Please note that Australian cup and spoon measurements are metric. A conversion chart appears on page 236.

With more than 60 million cookbooks sold, ACP Books is the publisher of some of the world's best-selling cookbooks. *The Australian Women's Weekly* cookbooks can be found from France to the Caribbean, and cooks as far afield as Dubai and Iceland have found them just as reliable as the cooks of Deniliquin and Auckland. Every book is prepared and presented with great expertise and attention to detail. Even more importantly, every single recipe is carefully tested, not once, but three times, in our famous Test Kitchen, giving you the reassuring guarantee that comes with all our cookbooks, wherever you are in the world – success first time, every time.

contents

I'm sure that most, if not all, of you can relate to this scenario: it's 5pm, you're stuck at work, and have no idea what to feed the starving hordes when you arrive home. Yes? Well, you're certainly not alone. I often find myself searching through the cupboard, trying to find inspiration, and I'm conscious that there are hungry tummies waiting. That's where this book comes in very handy; I know that I can flick to any page of the book and I'll be presented with a dinner option that is simple, quick and delicious – the perfect trifecta.

Pamela Clark

Food Director

seafood

salmon and roast potato salad

500g kipfler potatoes, chopped coarsely
425g can pink salmon
2 medium tomatoes (300g), cut into wedges
1 baby cos lettuce, torn roughly
½ cup (120g) sour cream
1 medium red onion (170g), chopped finely
¼ cup (50g) drained capers, chopped finely
2 tablespoons finely chopped fresh dill
2 tablespoons lemon juice

1 Preheat oven to 220°C/200°C fan-forced.
2 Place potato in lightly oiled large baking dish; roast, uncovered, about 30 minutes or until browned and crisp. Cool.
3 Drain salmon; remove any bones and skin, then flake with fork in large serving bowl.
4 Place cooled potato in bowl with salmon; add tomato and lettuce, toss to combine. Drizzle with combined remaining ingredients just before serving.

....

preparation time **10 minutes**
cooking time **30 minutes (plus cooling time)**
serves **4** per serving **17.6g fat; 1437kJ**

angel hair seafood laksa

500g medium uncooked prawns
1 tablespoon laksa paste
2 cups (500ml) vegetable stock
2 cups (500ml) water
400ml can coconut cream
300g firm white fish fillets, chopped coarsely
250g angel hair pasta
300g baby buk choy, chopped coarsely
4 green onions, sliced thinly
¼ cup loosely packed fresh coriander leaves

1 Shell and devein prawns, leaving tails intact.
2 Cook laksa paste in heated large saucepan, stirring, until fragrant. Stir in prawns, stock, the water, coconut cream and fish; bring to a boil. Reduce heat; simmer, uncovered, until fish is cooked.
3 Meanwhile, cook pasta in large saucepan of boiling water, uncovered, until just tender; drain.
4 Add buk choy, onion and coriander to laksa mixture; cook, uncovered, until buk choy is just wilted.
5 Divide pasta among serving bowls; top with laksa mixture.

preparation time **10 minutes** cooking time **15 minutes**
serves **4** per serving **23.9g fat; 2375kJ**
tip **This recipe is best made just before serving.**

We used ling fillets in this recipe but you can use any firm white fish fillet you like – or you can increase the amount of prawns called for and not use any fish.

linguine with crab

300g fresh crab meat
1 clove garlic, crushed
2 fresh small red thai chillies, sliced thinly
½ cup (125ml) dry white wine
1 tablespoon finely grated lemon rind
375g linguine
½ cup loosely packed fresh flat-leaf parsley,
    chopped coarsely
1 small red onion (100g), sliced thinly
⅓ cup (80ml) peanut oil

1 Cook crab, garlic and chilli in heated large frying pan, stirring, until crab is just cooked.
2 Add wine and rind; bring to a boil. Reduce heat; simmer, uncovered, until wine reduces by half.
3 Meanwhile, cook pasta in large saucepan of boiling water, uncovered, until just tender; drain.
4 Combine pasta in large bowl with crab mixture and remaining ingredients.

preparation time **10 minutes** cooking time **15 minutes**
serves **4** per serving **19.7g fat; 2299kJ**

snapper with a triple-cheese crust

1 tablespoon dijon mustard
1 cup (70g) stale breadcrumbs
⅓ cup (35g) coarsely grated
   mozzarella cheese
⅓ cup (40g) coarsely grated
   cheddar cheese
⅓ cup (25g) coarsely grated
   parmesan cheese
2 tablespoons finely chopped fresh parsley
2 cloves garlic, crushed
2 teaspoons lemon pepper seasoning
4 snapper fillets (800g)
cooking-oil spray

1 Preheat oven to 220°C/200°C fan-forced.
2 Combine mustard, breadcrumbs, cheeses, parsley, garlic and seasoning in large bowl.
3 Place fish on oiled oven tray; press cheese mixture onto fish, spray lightly with cooking oil. Bake, uncovered, about 20 minutes or until cheese browns and fish is cooked.

preparation time **10 minutes** cooking time **15 minutes**
serves **4** per serving **13.6g fat; 1572kJ**

We used snapper but you can use any firm white fish fillet.

spaghetti with prawns and coriander

250g spaghetti
40 medium uncooked prawns (1kg)
¼ cup (60ml) peanut oil
1 large red capsicum (350g), sliced thinly
⅓ cup (50g) raw unsalted coarsely
   chopped peanuts
⅓ cup (80ml) lime juice
2 tablespoons sweet chilli sauce
½ cup finely chopped fresh coriander

1 Cook pasta in large pan of boiling water, uncovered, until just tender; drain.
2 Meanwhile, shell and devein prawns, leaving tails intact.
3 Heat half the oil in wok or large frying pan; cook prawns, capsicum and nuts until prawns just change colour. Add pasta, remaining oil, juice, sauce and coriander to wok; stir-fry until hot.

preparation time **15 minutes** cooking time **15 minutes**
serves **4** per serving 21.4g fat; 2298kJ

north african-spiced fish with cucumber yogurt

1 lebanese cucumber (130g)
2 teaspoons ground coriander
2 teaspoons ground cumin
2 teaspoons grated fresh ginger
¼ cup (60ml) olive oil
4 white fish fillets (800g)
¾ cup (200g) yogurt
2 teaspoons finely chopped fresh mint
1 teaspoon finely grated lemon rind

1 Grate cucumber coarsely; drain in sieve 5 minutes.

2 Meanwhile, combine coriander, cumin, ginger and oil in small bowl. Brush fish with spice mixture; cook fish on heated oiled grill plate (or grill or barbecue) until cooked.

3 Combine cucumber with yogurt and mint in small bowl; serve fish drizzled with yogurt, then sprinkled with rind.

preparation time **10 minutes** cooking time **10 minutes**
serves **4** per serving **19.9g fat; 1532 kJ**

Serve fish with mixed lettuce leaves, if you like.

stir-fried scallops with hazelnuts

500g fresh scallops
2 teaspoons grated fresh ginger
1 clove garlic, crushed
1 tablespoon olive oil
1 medium brown onion (150g), sliced thinly
1 medium yellow capsicum (200g),
   sliced thinly
200g snow peas
1 tablespoon olive oil, extra
1 teaspoon cornflour
1 tablespoon light soy sauce
2 tablespoons finely chopped
   roasted hazelnuts

1 Combine scallops, ginger and garlic in bowl.
2 Heat oil in wok or large frying pan; stir-fry onion, capsicum and peas until onion is soft. Remove from pan.
3 Heat extra oil in wok; stir-fry scallop mixture until scallops are cooked. Return onion mixture to wok, stir in blended cornflour and sauce. Stir-fry over heat until mixture boils and thickens; stir in nuts. Serve with rice, if you like.

preparation time **10 minutes** cooking time **15 minutes**
serves **4** per serving **13.6g fat; 964kJ**

smoked salmon and spinach pizzas

½ cup (130g) bottled tomato pasta sauce
4 small pitta pocket breads
1 cup (125g) coarsely grated tasty cheese
¼ bunch spinach (75g), shredded finely
100g smoked salmon
1 small brown onion (80g), sliced thinly
2 teaspoons drained capers
1 cup (125g) coarsely grated tasty
   cheese, extra
1 teaspoon finely chopped fresh dill
¼ cup (60g) sour cream

1 Preheat oven to 180°C/160°C fan-forced.
2 Spread sauce evenly over pitta breads, place breads on oven tray. Sprinkle breads with cheese, spinach, salmon, onion and capers; sprinkle with extra cheese and dill.
3 Bake, uncovered, about 12 minutes or until cheese melts. Remove from oven; top with dollops of sour cream, then return to oven about 1 minute or until cream is warm. Serve with salad, if you like.

preparation time **10 minutes** cooking time **15 minutes**
serves **4** per serving **29.4g fat; 1957kJ**

trout with creamy sun-dried tomato sauce

4 rainbow trout (1kg)
30g butter, melted
1 clove garlic, crushed
½ cup (75g) drained sun-dried tomatoes in
    oil, chopped coarsely
⅔ cup (160ml) thickened cream
1 tablespoon lime juice
1 teaspoon cornflour
¼ cup (60ml) water

1 Preheat oven to 180°C/160°C fan-forced.
2 Place trout in single layer in oiled large ovenproof dish, brush with butter. Bake, uncovered, about 20 minutes or until cooked.
3 Meanwhile, heat garlic and tomato in small saucepan. Stir in cream, juice and blended cornflour and the water; stir over heat until mixture boils and thickens. Serve fish drizzled with sauce, and steamed vegetables, if you like.

preparation time **5 minutes** cooking time **20 minutes**
serves **4** per serving 27.9g fat; 1779kJ
tip Sauce can be prepared a day ahead.

seafood stew

2 tablespoons olive oil
1 large brown onion (200g), chopped finely
2 cloves garlic, crushed
410g can crushed tomatoes
¼ cup (60ml) dry red wine
¼ cup (60g) tomato paste
1 tablespoon brown sugar
1 tablespoon balsamic vinegar
½ cup (125ml) water
1kg marinara mix
2 tablespoons coarsely chopped
    fresh oregano

1 Heat oil in large saucepan; cook onion and garlic, stirring, until onion is soft. Add undrained tomatoes, wine, paste, sugar, vinegar and the water; bring to a boil. Reduce heat; simmer, uncovered, about 20 minutes or until sauce thickens. [Can be prepared ahead to this point; refrigerate for up to 2 days or freeze]

2 Add seafood to pan; simmer, uncovered, about 10 minutes or until seafood is cooked. Stir in oregano just before serving.

preparation time **5 minutes** cooking time **40 minutes**
serves **4** per serving **16.7g fat; 1993kJ**

greek barbecued octopus salad

Capture the essence of an Aegean summer with this flavour-packed Greek-style salad.

⅓ cup (80ml) lemon juice
1 tablespoon honey
4 cloves garlic, crushed
¼ teaspoon cayenne pepper
1kg cleaned baby octopus, halved
100g baby spinach leaves
1 small red onion (100g), sliced thinly
250g cherry tomatoes, halved
1 tablespoon finely shredded fresh
    mint leaves
1 tablespoon finely shredded fresh
    basil leaves
100g fetta cheese, chopped coarsely

1 Combine juice, honey, garlic, pepper and octopus in large bowl, cover; refrigerate 3 hours or overnight.

2 Drain octopus over large bowl; reserve marinade. Cook octopus, in batches, on heated oiled grill plate (or barbecue or grill) until tender.

3 Meanwhile, bring reserved marinade to a boil in small saucepan. Reduce heat; simmer, uncovered, about 5 minutes or until marinade reduces slightly. Cool.

4 Just before serving, combine octopus and marinade in large bowl with remaining ingredients.

preparation time **10 minutes (plus refrigeration time)**
cooking time **10 minutes (plus cooling time)**
serves **4** per serving **8.6g fat; 1278kJ**
tip **Substitute rocket or any other salad green for the spinach.**
serving suggestion **Serve with a bowl of tzatziki, the piquant Greek combination of cucumber, yogurt and garlic.**

salmon and dill pie with horseradish sauce

A fish or cabbage pie, coulibiac was originally a Russian peasant dish that was adopted and refined by the French. Our version is simpler than the traditional one but no less delicious.

2 teaspoons olive oil
2 small leeks (400g), sliced thinly
1 cup (80g) finely grated parmesan cheese
1 cup (70g) stale breadcrumbs, toasted
2 tablespoons finely chopped fresh dill
4 salmon fillets (800g)
4 sheets frozen puff pastry, thawed
cooking-oil spray
horseradish sauce
2 teaspoons olive oil
1 medium brown onion (150g),
   chopped finely
1 tablespoon horseradish cream
300ml cream
2 tablespoons finely chopped fresh dill

1 Heat oil in medium frying pan; cook leek, stirring, until soft. Remove from heat; stir in cheese, breadcrumbs and dill.
2 Halve salmon fillets horizontally. Halve pastry sheets; cut corners of each half to make oval shapes. Place about ¼ cup leek mixture on 1 piece pastry, leaving a 2cm border; top with 1 piece salmon, then another ¼ cup leek mixture and another piece salmon. Brush edges of pastry with water, place 1 piece pastry over salmon; turn up bottom edges and press with fork to enclose filling.
3 Repeat process with remaining leek mixture, pastry and salmon pieces.
4 Preheat oven to 220°C/200°C fan-forced.
5 Place pies on oiled oven trays; spray with cooking oil. Bake, uncovered, about 20 minutes or until browned lightly and heated through.
6 Meanwhile, make horseradish sauce.
7 Serve pie with horseradish sauce.
horseradish sauce Heat oil in small saucepan; cook onion, stirring, until browned lightly. Add horseradish and cream. Bring to boil; simmer, stirring, about 1 minute or until mixture thickens slightly and is heated through. Just before serving, stir in dill.

preparation time **25 minutes** cooking time **30 minutes** serves **4** per serving 98g fat; 6062kJ

kaffir lime and lemon grass fish parcels

If you can't buy kaffir lime leaves, substitute the young leaves from any other citrus tree.

200g rice stick noodles
4 bream fillets (600g)
150g baby buk choy, quartered
150g snow peas, sliced thinly lengthways
1 tablespoon thinly sliced lemon grass
8 kaffir lime leaves, torn
1 teaspoon japanese soy sauce
2 tablespoons sweet chilli sauce
1 teaspoon fish sauce
2 tablespoons lime juice
1 tablespoon coarsely chopped
  fresh coriander

1 Preheat oven to 220°C/200°C fan-forced.
2 Place noodles in large heatproof bowl, cover with boiling water, stand until just tender; drain.
3 Divide noodles into four equal portions; place each on a large piece of foil. Top noodles with fish; top fish with equal amounts of buk choy, snow peas, lemon grass and lime leaves. Drizzle with combined sauces and juice. Enclose fish stacks in foil; place in single layer on oven tray.
4 Cook parcels about 15 minutes or until fish is cooked; open foil and transfer stacks to serving plates. Sprinkle with coriander.

preparation time **10 minutes** cooking time **15 minutes**
serves **4** per serving **4.4g fat; 1393kJ**
serving suggestion **Serve with wedges of lime or fresh grapefruit segments.**
tip **Fish parcels can be assembled several hours ahead; store in refrigerator.**

fish with spicy tomato and olive sauce

¼ cup (60ml) olive oil
1 medium brown onion (150g),
   chopped finely
2 cloves garlic, crushed
1 teaspoon sambal oelek
410g can crushed tomatoes
¼ cup (60ml) dry red wine
½ cup (60g) seeded black olives
8 anchovy fillets, drained, chopped finely
1 tablespoon drained capers
1 teaspoon sugar
1 teaspoon cracked black peppercorns
4 white fish cutlets (800g)

1 Heat oil in large frying pan; add onion and garlic, cook, stirring, until onion is soft. Stir in sambal oelek, undrained tomatoes and wine; bring to a boil. Reduce heat; simmer, uncovered, about 2 minutes or until sauce thickens slightly. Add olives, anchovy, capers, sugar and pepper; stir until hot.

2 Meanwhile, cook fish on heated oiled grill plate (or grill or barbecue) until cooked. Serve fish topped with sauce.

preparation time **5 minutes** cooking time **10 minutes**
serves **4** per serving **18.3g fat; 1532 kJ**

chicken

chicken broth with rice noodles

You'll find a version of this popular soup in most Asian cuisines; this one has a Thai accent.

1.5 litres (6 cups) chicken stock
2 cups (500ml) water
10cm piece fresh ginger (50g), sliced thinly
350g chicken breast fillets
500g fresh rice noodles
¼ cup (60ml) lime juice
1 tablespoon fish sauce
4 green onions, chopped coarsely
2 fresh small red thai chillies, sliced thinly
2 tablespoons coarsely chopped
   fresh coriander
1 cup (80g) bean sprouts

1 Bring stock, the water and ginger to a boil in large saucepan. Add chicken; simmer, covered, about 15 minutes or until chicken is cooked. Remove chicken; cool 10 minutes, then shred coarsely.
2 Return broth mixture to a boil; add noodles, juice and sauce. Reduce heat; simmer, stirring, until noodles are just tender.
3 Add chicken and remaining ingredients to broth; stir over heat until hot.

preparation time **15 minutes**
cooking time **25 minutes (plus cooling time)**
serves **4** per serving **7.4g fat; 1711kJ**
tip **Coarsely chopped leafy green Chinese vegetables, such as choy sum or water spinach, can be added to this broth.**

Dried rice noodles, or the thicker rice stick noodles, can be substituted for fresh noodles; they need to be soaked in boiling water for about 5 minutes and drained before being added to the stock.

chicken, oyster-mushroom and broccoli stir-fry

You will need about 500g of broccoli for this recipe. Hokkien (or stir-fry) noodles are sold in cryovac packages in the refrigerated section of your supermarket.

500g hokkien noodles
500g chicken thigh fillets, chopped coarsely
1 clove garlic, crushed
1 cup (250g) broccoli florets
150g oyster mushrooms, halved
1 medium red onion (170g), sliced thinly
200g snow peas, halved lengthways
¼ cup (60ml) oyster sauce

1 Place noodles in large heatproof bowl, cover with boiling water, stand until just tender; drain.

2 Stir-fry chicken in heated oiled wok or large frying pan, in batches, until cooked.

3 Stir-fry garlic, broccoli, mushrooms and onion in wok until onion is soft. Return chicken to wok with noodles, snow peas and sauce; stir-fry until hot.

preparation time 15 minutes cooking time 15 minutes
serves 4 per serving 10.9g fat; 2360kJ
serving suggestion Serve with a side dish of chopped fresh chilli or sambal oelek to add heat to the noodles.

chicken with lentil salsa

The spices of North Africa give the chicken a flavour-packed jolt in this dish. And, as it can be served hot or cold, this recipe is a good prepare-ahead dish.

2 teaspoons ground cumin
2 teaspoons ground coriander
1 teaspoon ground turmeric
12 chicken tenderloins (900g)
1½ cups (300g) red lentils
1 clove garlic, crushed
1 fresh small red thai chilli, chopped finely
1 lebanese cucumber (130g), seeded, chopped finely
1 medium red capsicum (200g), chopped finely
¼ cup (60ml) lemon juice
2 teaspoons peanut oil
2 tablespoons coarsely chopped fresh coriander leaves
2 limes, cut into wedges

1 Combine spices and tenderloins in medium bowl.
2 Cook lentils in large saucepan of boiling water, uncovered, until just tender; drain. Rinse under cold water; drain. Place lentils in large bowl with garlic, chilli, cucumber, capsicum, juice, oil and fresh coriander.
3 Meanwhile, cook chicken on heated lightly oiled grill plate (or grill or barbecue) until cooked. Add limes to pan; cook until browned both sides. Serve chicken with lentil salsa and lime wedges.

preparation time **10 minutes** cooking time **15 minutes**
serves **4** per serving **16.8g fat; 2314kJ**
tip **You could add 1 teaspoon of harissa to the salad instead of the chilli**
serving suggestion **Serve accompanied with lavash bread, if you like.**

chicken kibbeh burger

This recipe combines favourite Middle-Eastern flavours in the chicken patties. Burghul is made from steamed, dried and crushed wheat kernels.

⅓ cup (55g) burghul
500g chicken mince
⅓ cup loosely packed fresh flat-leaf parsley, chopped coarsely
1 small red onion (100g), chopped finely
2 teaspoons finely grated lemon rind
1 tablespoon lemon juice
1 egg white, beaten lightly
4 small wholemeal pocket pitta bread
2 medium tomatoes (300g), sliced thickly
8 baby cos lettuce leaves

lemon mayonnaise
⅓ cup (100g) low-fat mayonnaise
2 tablespoons lemon juice
1 clove garlic, crushed

1 Place burghul in small bowl; cover with cold water. Stand 10 minutes; drain. Using hands, squeeze out excess water.
2 Combine chicken, parsley, onion, rind, juice and egg white in large bowl. Stir in burghul; using one hand, work in burghul to form a smooth paste. Shape chicken mixture into four patties.
3 Cook patties in heated oiled large frying pan, uncovered, until cooked.
4 Meanwhile, make lemon mayonnaise.
5 Split pitta; divide tomato, lettuce and patties among pockets. Drizzle burgers with lemon mayonnaise.

lemon mayonnaise Combine ingredients in small bowl.

preparation time **15 minutes (plus standing time)**
cooking time **10 minutes**
serves **4** per serving **15.1g fat; 2208kJ**
tip **Chicken patties can be made in advance and frozen. Lemon mayonnaise can be made a day ahead, too; store, covered, in refrigerator.**
serving suggestion **You can replace the lemon mayonnaise with a dollop of hummus, if you like.**

chicken, asparagus and potato casserole

1 tablespoon peanut oil
6 shallots (150g), quartered
2 cloves garlic, crushed
700g chicken thigh fillets, chopped coarsely
300g baby new potatoes, quartered
1 large carrot (180g), chopped coarsely
¼ cup (35g) plain flour
⅓ cup (80ml) dry white wine
420g can chicken consomme
500g asparagus, trimmed, halved crossways
2 tablespoons wholegrain mustard
1 tablespoon finely grated lemon rind
⅓ cup loosely packed fresh flat-leaf parsley,
    chopped coarsely

1 Heat oil in large saucepan; cook shallots and garlic, stirring, until shallots is soft. Add chicken; cook, stirring, about 5 minutes or until chicken is browned.
2 Add potato, carrot and flour to pan; cook, stirring, 5 minutes. Add wine and consomme; cook, stirring, until mixture boils and thickens. Simmer, covered, about 10 minutes or until potato is tender.
3 Add asparagus, mustard and rind; bring to a boil. Reduce heat; simmer, covered, until asparagus is just tender. Stir in parsley.

preparation time **15 minutes** cooking time **30 minutes**
serves **4** per serving **17.4g fat; 1746kJ**
tip **This recipe is more flavoursome if made a day ahead; store, covered, in refrigerator. Reheat just before serving.**

chicken and fennel spirals

2 medium fennel bulbs (600g), trimmed,
    sliced thinly
3 cloves garlic, sliced thinly
¼ cup (60ml) dry sherry
1½ cups (375ml) chicken stock
375g large pasta spirals
2 cups (320g) shredded cooked chicken
200g snow peas, trimmed, sliced
    thinly lengthways
1 cup (240g) sour cream
1 tablespoon coarsely chopped
    fresh tarragon

1 Preheat oven to 240°C/220°C fan-forced.
2 Combine fennel, garlic, sherry and ½ cup
of the stock in large baking dish; roast,
uncovered, about 15 minutes or until fennel
is just tender.
3 Meanwhile, cook pasta in large saucepan
of boiling water, uncovered, until just
tender; drain.
4 Place fennel mixture and pasta in same
cleaned pan with remaining ingredients; stir
until hot.

preparation time **10 minutes** cooking time **20 minutes**
serves **4** per serving **31.5g fat; 3106kJ**

honey-mustard chicken with potato kumara mash

Soak eight bamboo skewers in water for at least an hour before use to prevent them from splintering and/or scorching. The honey-mustard marinade is also used to make the sauce in this recipe.

8 chicken tenderloins (600g)
⅓ cup (115g) honey
2 tablespoons wholegrain mustard
⅓ cup (80ml) white vinegar
2 tablespoons japanese soy sauce
3 medium potatoes (600g)
1 small kumara (250g)
2 cloves garlic, sliced thinly
¼ cup (60ml) skim milk
2 teaspoons fresh thyme leaves

1 Thread chicken onto skewers; place in large shallow baking dish. Pour half the combined honey, mustard, vinegar and sauce over chicken, cover; refrigerate 3 hours or overnight.
2 Preheat oven to 220°C/200°C fan-forced.
3 Roast undrained chicken, uncovered, about 10 minutes or until cooked.
4 Meanwhile, boil, steam or microwave combined potato, kumara and garlic until tender; drain. Mash in medium bowl with milk; stir in thyme.
5 Heat remaining marinade in small saucepan. Serve chicken with potato kumara mash; drizzle with marinade.

preparation time **15 minutes (plus refrigeration time)**
cooking time **15 minutes**
serves **4** per serving **8.7g fat; 1842kJ**
tip Grill or barbecue the chicken rather than baking it, if you like.

braised spatchcock with choy sum and potatoes

4 x 500g spatchcock
2 teaspoons finely grated lime rind
¼ cup (60ml) lime juice
2 teaspoons sweet chilli sauce
3 cloves garlic, crushed
500g baby new potatoes, unpeeled, halved
2 tablespoons peanut oil
600g choy sum, chopped coarsely
2 tablespoons lime juice, extra
1 tablespoon finely chopped fresh coriander

1 Cut along both sides of spatchcock back-bones; discard backbones. Cut along breast bones, dividing spatchcock in half.
2 Place spatchcock in large saucepan of boiling water. Reduce heat; simmer, uncovered, 10 minutes. Remove spatchcock from pan; place, in single layer, in shallow large baking dish. Discard cooking liquid.
3 Combine rind, juice, sauce and garlic in small jug; pour over spatchcock. Cover; refrigerate 3 hours. [Can be prepared ahead to this point; refrigerate overnight or freeze]
4 Drain spatchcock; reserve marinade. Cook spatchcock, in batches, in heated oiled large frying pan until cooked, brushing occasionally with reserved marinade. Cover to keep warm.
5 Meanwhile, boil, steam or microwave potatoes until just tender; drain. Heat 1 tablespoon of the oil in medium frying pan; add potato, cook until browned. Add choy sum; cook, stirring, until just wilted.
6 Drizzle spatchcock with combined remaining oil, extra juice and coriander; serve with potato and choy sum mixture.

preparation time **20 minutes (plus refrigeration time)**
cooking time **25 minutes**
serves **4** per serving **49.2g fat; 3088kJ**

pad thai

Noodles are a favourite Thai snack, and for this dish they usually use sen lek, a 5mm-wide rice stick noodle.

250g rice stick noodles
450g chicken thigh fillets, sliced thinly
1 clove garlic, crushed
1 teaspoon grated fresh ginger
2 fresh small red thai chillies, sliced thinly
2 tablespoons palm sugar
2 tablespoons japanese soy sauce
¼ cup (60ml) sweet chilli sauce
1 tablespoon fish sauce
1 tablespoon lime juice
3 green onions, sliced thinly
1 cup (80g) bean sprouts
1 cup (80g) snow pea sprouts
¼ cup coarsely chopped fresh coriander

1 Place noodles in large heatproof bowl, cover with boiling water, stand until just tender; drain.
2 Stir-fry chicken, garlic, ginger and chilli in heated wok or large frying pan, in batches, until chicken is browned.
3 Return chicken mixture to wok with sugar, sauces and juice; stir-fry until sauce thickens slightly. Add noodles, onion and sprouts to wok; stir-fry until hot. Serve pad thai sprinkled with coriander.

preparation time **15 minutes** cooking time **15 minutes**
serves **4** per serving **9.2g fat; 1717kJ**
tip **Remove seeds from chilli if you prefer a milder flavour.**

Palm sugar, also sold as jaggery, is a product of the coconut palm. Substitute black or brown sugar if you can't find palm sugar at your supermarket.

moroccan chicken

2 tablespoons olive oil
1.5kg chicken pieces
1 large brown onion (200g), sliced thinly
2 cloves garlic, crushed
2 cinnamon sticks
2 teaspoons ground cumin
2 teaspoons ground turmeric
2 x 6cm strips lemon rind
⅓ cup (80ml) lemon juice
410g can crushed tomatoes
½ cup (125ml) water
½ cup (60g) seeded black olives

1 Heat oil in large saucepan; cook chicken, in batches, until browned. Drain; cover to keep warm.
2 Add onion, garlic, cinnamon and ground spices to same pan; cook, stirring, until onion is soft. Return chicken to pan with rind, juice, undrained crushed tomatoes and water. Bring to boil; simmer, covered, about 40 minutes or until chicken is cooked through. [Can be prepared ahead to this point; refrigerate up to 2 days or freeze]
3 Stir in olives; simmer, uncovered, about 10 minutes or until sauce thickens slightly. Discard cinnamon sticks. Serve with couscous and lemon wedges, if you like.

preparation time **10 minutes**
cooking time **1 hour 15 minutes**
serves **4** per serving **44.5g fat; 2600kJ**

lemon tarragon chicken

80g butter, softened
1 tablespoon finely grated lemon rind
1 tablespoon lemon juice
1 tablespoon finely chopped fresh tarragon
1 tablespoon brown sugar
4 chicken breast fillets (800g)
1 lemon, sliced thinly
8 garlic cloves, unpeeled

1 Preheat oven to 220°C/200°C fan-forced.

2 Combine butter, rind, juice, tarragon and sugar in small bowl. Make 3 deep diagonal cuts across each piece of chicken. Press half the butter mixture into cuts; spread remainder over chicken. Place chicken in shallow large baking dish, in single layer, with lemon and garlic.

3 Bake, uncovered, about 20 minutes or until chicken is cooked. Serve with grilled tomato and steamed greens, if you like.

preparation time **15 minutes** cooking time **20 minutes**
serves **4** per serving **27.6g fat; 1843 kJ**

chicken, kumara and fetta bake

250g fetta cheese
250g packet frozen spinach, thawed
2 large kumara (1kg), sliced thinly
680g chicken breast fillets, sliced thinly
1 large brown onion (200g), chopped finely
2 teaspoons finely chopped fresh thyme
¼ cup (60g) light sour cream
½ cup (125ml) chicken stock
2 teaspoons plain flour
1 tablespoon water
2 cups (250g) coarsely grated pizza cheese

1 Crumble fetta into medium bowl. Using hands, squeeze excess moisture from spinach; combine spinach with fetta.
2 Boil, steam or microwave kumara until just tender; drain.
3 Meanwhile, cook chicken, in batches, in heated oiled medium frying pan until browned.
4 Cook onion and thyme in same cleaned pan, stirring, until onion is soft; stir onion into fetta mixture.
5 Cook cream, stock and blended flour and water in same cleaned pan, stirring, until mixture boils and thickens.
6 Preheat oven to 180°C/160°C fan-forced.
7 Place half the kumara, half the chicken and all of the fetta mixture, in layers, in oiled 3-litre (12-cup) ovenproof dish. Repeat layering with remaining kumara and chicken; pour cream mixture over the top. [Can be prepared ahead to this point; refrigerate overnight or freeze] Sprinkle with pizza cheese; bake, uncovered, about 30 minutes or until cheese melts and top browns lightly.

preparation time **20 minutes** cooking time **50 minutes**
serves **4** per serving **44.2g fat; 3502kJ**

couscous chicken with fresh corn salsa

Couscous, the North African cereal made from semolina, lends an intriguing crunch to the coating on the chicken.

½ teaspoon ground cumin
¼ teaspoon ground coriander
¼ teaspoon garam masala
¼ teaspoon ground turmeric
1 cup (250ml) chicken stock
1 cup (200g) couscous
700g chicken breast fillets
1 egg white, beaten lightly
2 trimmed corn cobs (500g)
2 medium tomatoes (300g), seeded, chopped coarsely
1 small avocado (200g), chopped coarsely
2 tablespoons red wine vinegar
4 green onions, chopped finely

1 Preheat oven to 200°C/180°C fan-forced.
2 Cook spices in heated medium saucepan, stirring, until fragrant. Add stock; bring to a boil. Stir in couscous; remove from heat, stand, covered, about 5 minutes or until stock is absorbed, fluffing with fork occasionally to separate grains.
3 Dip chicken in egg white; coat firmly in couscous. Place chicken, in single layer, in lightly oiled large baking dish; bake, uncovered, about 10 minutes or until chicken is cooked. Cover to keep warm.
4 Meanwhile, remove kernels from corn cobs. Cook kernels in small pan of boiling water, uncovered, about 2 minutes or until just tender; drain. Rinse under cold water; drain. Combine corn with remaining ingredients in medium bowl. Serve corn salsa with thickly sliced chicken.

preparation time **15 minutes**
cooking time **12 minutes (plus standing time)**
serves **4** per serving **19.1g fat; 2515kJ**
tip The salsa, without the avocado, can be prepared about 3 hours ahead; store, covered, in refrigerator. Add avocado just before serving.
serving suggestion Add coarsely chopped fresh coriander or finely chopped fresh chilli to the corn salsa. Serve with snow pea sprouts, if you like.

satay chicken burgers

Turkish bread can be found on the breadshelves of your favourite supermarket but, if at all possible, try a loaf freshly baked from a Middle-Eastern bakery — it's absolutely delicious!

1 large turkish bread (430g)
750g chicken mince
1 cup (70g) stale breadcrumbs
¼ cup finely chopped fresh coriander
⅔ cup (200g) satay sauce
1 large carrot (180g), peeled
1 lebanese cucumber (130g)
1 cup (280g) yogurt

1 Quarter turkish bread widthways; cut each piece in half horizontally. Place pieces, cut-side up, on oven tray; grill under preheated grill until browned lightly.
2 Combine chicken, breadcrumbs, coriander and half the sauce in large bowl. Using hand, shape mixture into four patties. Cook in heated oiled large frying pan until cooked.
3 Meanwhile, using a vegetable peeler, slice carrot and cucumber into thin strips.
4 Combine remaining sauce and yogurt in small bowl. Divide half the satay yogurt among bread bases, top with patties, carrot and cucumber. Drizzle burgers with remaining satay yogurt, then top with remaining bread pieces.

preparation time **15 minutes** cooking time **10 minutes**
serves **4** per serving **33.7g fat; 3573kJ**

warm chicken and potato salad

2 tablespoons olive oil
1kg baby new potatoes, halved
4 rindless bacon rashers (260g),
    chopped coarsely
1 barbecued chicken (900g)
½ cup (120g) sour cream
⅓ cup (100g) mayonnaise
2 tablespoons wholegrain mustard
¼ cup finely chopped fresh chives

1 Preheat oven to 220°C/200°C fan-forced.
2 Combine oil and potato in large baking dish; roast, uncovered, 25 minutes, turning once during cooking.
3 Meanwhile, cook bacon in heated oiled large frying pan until crisp; drain on absorbent paper.
4 Remove and discard skin and bones from chicken; chop chicken coarsely.
5 Combine potato, bacon and chicken in large bowl with remaining ingredients.

preparation time **10 minutes** cooking time **25 minutes**
serves **4** per serving **55.2g fat; 4026kJ**

peppercorn chicken

8 chicken thigh cutlets (1.2kg)
¼ cup (60g) wholegrain mustard
2 tablespoons drained green peppercorns,
    chopped coarsely
2 cloves garlic, crushed
2 tablespoons lemon juice
¼ cup chopped fresh chives
¼ cup (60ml) olive oil
1 small brown onion (80g), chopped finely

1 Remove and discard skin from chicken; combine chicken in large bowl with mustard, peppercorns, garlic, juice, chives and 2 tablespoons of the oil.

2 Heat remaining oil in large frying pan; cook onion, stirring, until soft. Add chicken to pan; cook, brushing occasionally with peppercorn mixture, until chicken is cooked. Serve with pasta salad and lemon wedges, if you like.

preparation time **10 minutes** cooking time **15 minutes**
serves **4** per serving **20.7g fat; 1742kJ**

spiced chicken with kashmiri pilaf

While many Indian dishes involve long, slow cooking, this recipe captures the essence of the cuisine in a quick and easy char-grill.

1 tablespoon vegetable oil
1 small brown onion (80g), chopped finely
1 clove garlic, crushed
1 teaspoon black mustard seeds
¼ teaspoon ground cardamom
½ teaspoon ground cumin
½ teaspoon garam masala
½ teaspoon ground turmeric
1½ cups (300g) white long-grain rice
3 cups (750ml) chicken stock
2 tablespoons coarsely chopped
   fresh coriander
⅓ cup (80g) mango chutney
2 tablespoons water
680g chicken breast fillets

1 Heat oil in medium saucepan; cook onion, garlic and mustard seeds, stirring, until onion is soft and seeds pop. Add remaining spices; cook, stirring, until fragrant.
2 Add rice; stir to coat in spices. Add stock; bring to a boil. Reduce heat; simmer, uncovered, until rice is just tender. Stir in coriander; cover to keep warm.
3 Meanwhile, combine chutney with the water in small saucepan; cook, stirring, until heated through.
4 Cook chicken, brushing occasionally with chutney mixture, on heated oiled grill plate (or grill or barbecue) until cooked. Cut into thick slices. Serve chutney chicken with pilaf. Sprinkle with extra coriander leaves, if you like.

preparation time **5 minutes**
cooking time **25 minutes (plus standing time)**
serves **4** per serving **15.3g fat; 2561kJ**
tip Mango chutney will burn if the grill or barbecue is too hot.

chicken, hazelnut and rocket salad

250g linguine
340g chicken breast fillets
½ cup (75g) roasted hazelnuts,
    chopped coarsely
100g curly endive, trimmed
150g baby rocket leaves
⅓ cup (80ml) lime juice
⅓ cup (80ml) olive oil
2 cloves garlic, crushed
2 teaspoons dijon mustard

1 Cook pasta in large saucepan of boiling water, uncovered, until just tender; drain. Rinse pasta under cold water; drain.
2 Meanwhile, cook chicken on heated oiled grill plate (or grill or barbecue) until cooked. Stand 5 minutes; slice thinly.
3 Combine pasta and chicken in large bowl with nuts, endive, rocket and combined remaining ingredients.

preparation time **5 minutes** cooking time **15 minutes**
serves **4** per serving **35.6g fat; 2593kJ**

beef & veal

lemon grass beef stir-fry

Rice stick noodles, also known as sen lek (Thai) and ho fun (Chinese), are wide, flat noodles made from rice flour. They must be softened by being soaked in boiling water before use.

250g rice stick noodles
2 teaspoons peanut oil
500g beef eye fillet, sliced thinly
1 clove garlic, crushed
1 tablespoon finely chopped lemon grass
2 fresh small red thai chillies, sliced thinly
⅓ cup (80ml) lime juice
1 tablespoon fish sauce
100g baby rocket leaves
1 cup (80g) bean sprouts
½ cup loosely packed fresh coriander leaves
½ cup loosely packed fresh mint leaves
3 green onions, sliced thinly
1 lebanese cucumber (130g), seeded, sliced thinly

1 Place noodles in large heatproof bowl, cover with boiling water, stand until just tender; drain.
2 Heat half the oil in wok or large frying pan; cook beef, in batches, until browned.
3 Heat remaining oil in wok; cook garlic, lemon grass and chilli until fragrant. Return beef to wok with juice and sauce, stir-fry until hot. Add noodles, stir-fry until combined. Stir in remaining ingredients; serve immediately.

preparation time **15 minutes (plus soaking time)**
cooking time **20 minutes**
serves **4** per serving **9.5g fat; 1534kj**
tip **Substitute baby spinach leaves, chinese water spinach or baby tat soi leaves for the rocket.**
serving suggestion **Serve with wedges of lime and a bowl of finely chopped chilli.**

sausage and bean hot pot

500g thin beef sausages
1 medium brown onion (150g), sliced thinly
440g can baked beans
2 tablespoons tomato paste
410g can crushed tomatoes
1 tablespoon finely chopped fresh
    flat-leaf parsley

1 Cook sausages in large frying pan until cooked. Drain on absorbent paper; slice thickly.

2 Add onion to same pan; cook, stirring, until onion is soft.

3 Return sausages to pan with undrained beans, paste and undrained tomatoes; stir until hot. Serve sprinkled with parsley; accompany with mashed potatoes and creamed corn, if you like.

preparation time **5 minutes** cooking time **20 minutes**
serves **4** per serving **33.9g; 1937kJ**
tip **Recipe can be prepared a day ahead and refrigerated, covered.**

rissoles with cabbage mash

2 rindless bacon rashers (130g),
   chopped finely
1 small brown onion (80g), chopped finely
1 clove garlic, crushed
1 fresh small red thai chilli, chopped finely
1 tablespoon worcestershire sauce
1 cup (70g) stale breadcrumbs
1 egg
¼ cup coarsely chopped fresh
   flat-leaf parsley
500g beef mince
2 tablespoons barbecue sauce
1 tablespoon vegetable oil
1 tablespoon dijon mustard
2 cups (500ml) beef stock
1 tablespoon cornflour
2 tablespoons water
cabbage mash
1kg potatoes, quartered
¼ cup (60ml) cream
30g butter, chopped
200g finely shredded savoy cabbage
1 small white onion (80g), chopped finely

1 Make cabbage mash.
2 Meanwhile, cook bacon, onion, garlic and chilli in medium frying pan, stirring, until onion is soft. Remove from heat.
3 Combine worcestershire, breadcrumbs, egg, parsley, mince and half the barbecue sauce with bacon mixture in large bowl; using hand, shape mixture into eight rissoles.
4 Heat oil in same pan; cook rissoles, in batches, until cooked. Cover to keep warm.
5 Place mustard, stock and remaining barbecue sauce in same pan; bring to a boil. Stir in blended cornflour and water; cook, stirring, until gravy boils and thickens slightly.
6 Serve rissoles, topped with gravy, with cabbage mash.

cabbage mash Boil, steam or microwave potato until tender; drain. Mash potato with cream and butter until smooth; stir in cabbage and onion. Cover to keep warm.

preparation time **25 minutes** cooking time **20 minutes**
serves **4** per serving **35.9g fat; 3038kJ**
tip Rissoles can be prepared a day ahead and kept, covered, in the refrigerator.

veal with potato pea mash

There's not a hint of deprivation in this satisfying combination of veal and mash.

450g veal steaks
⅓ cup (50g) plain flour
1 egg white, beaten lightly
2 tablespoons skim milk
1 cup (160g) cornflake crumbs
1 teaspoon finely grated lemon rind
2 tablespoons finely chopped fresh
   flat-leaf parsley
cooking-oil spray
4 medium potatoes (800g)
¼ cup (60ml) buttermilk
¾ cup (180ml) chicken stock
2 cups (250g) frozen peas

1 Preheat oven to 240°C/220°C fan-forced.

2 Cut each steak in half. Toss veal in flour; shake away excess flour. Coat veal in combined egg white and milk, then in combined crumbs, rind and parsley.

3 Place veal, in single layer, on lightly oiled oven tray; spray with cooking-oil. Bake, uncovered, about 5 minutes or until cooked. Stand 5 minutes; slice thickly.

4 Meanwhile, boil, steam or microwave potatoes until soft; drain. Mash potatoes with buttermilk in medium bowl; cover to keep warm.

5 Place stock in medium saucepan; bring to a boil. Add peas; cook, uncovered, until stock reduces by half. Blend or process pea mixture until almost smooth.

6 Swirl pea mixture into potato mash to give marbled effect. Divide potato and pea mash among plates; top with veal.

preparation time **10 minutes** cooking time **20 minutes**
serves 4 per serving 4.3g fat; 2154kJ
tip **Veal can be crumbed several hours ahead; store, covered, in refrigerator.**

veal cutlets with lemon mustard butter

¼ cup (60ml) lemon juice
2 tablespoons olive oil
1 tablespoon balsamic vinegar
2 cloves garlic, crushed
4 veal cutlets (500g)
lemon mustard butter
125g butter
1 tablespoon wholegrain mustard
1 tablespoon finely chopped
  sun-dried tomatoes
1 tablespoon finely chopped fresh
  flat-leaf parsley
1 teaspoon finely grated lemon rind

1 Combine juice, oil, vinegar, garlic and cutlets in large bowl. Cover; refrigerate 3 hours or overnight. [Can be prepared ahead to this point and frozen]

2 Drain cutlets; reserve lemon mixture. Cook cutlets on heated oiled grill plate (or grill or barbecue) until cooked as desired, brushing occasionally with lemon marinade. Serve with lemon mustard butter, and roasted potatoes, if you like.

lemon mustard butter Combine ingredients in small bowl. Place mixture on baking paper; roll into log shape. Wrap log in plastic.

preparation time **20 minutes (plus refrigeration time)**
cooking time **10 minutes**
serves **4** per serving **37.3g fat; 1808kJ**

beef with almond, mint and lemon

1 tablespoon vegetable oil
1 large brown onion (200g), sliced thickly
2 teaspoons ground cumin
1 teaspoon finely grated lemon rind
410g can crushed tomatoes
750g beef strips
2 tablespoons slivered almonds, roasted
2 teaspoons finely shredded fresh mint

1 Heat oil in large frying pan; cook onion, stirring, until soft. Add cumin and rind to pan; cook until fragrant. Stir in undrained tomatoes, bring to boil. Reduce heat; simmer, stirring occasionally, about 5 minutes or until mixture thickens slightly.

2 Meanwhile, cook beef, in batches, in another heated oiled large frying pan until cooked.

3 Add tomato mixture and remaining ingredients to beef; stir to combine.

preparation time **5 minutes** cooking time **15 minutes**
serves **4** per serving **20.2g fat; 1628kJ**

mustard veal with polenta and spinach puree

Polenta is the Italian answer to mashed potato – the perfect accompaniment for soaking up meat juices and too-good-to-waste sauces.

⅓ cup (95g) seeded mustard
2 tablespoons coarsely chopped
    fresh oregano
2 cloves garlic, crushed
4 veal chops (800g)
4 large egg tomatoes (360g), halved
2 cups (500ml) water
1 teaspoon salt
1 cup (170g) polenta
¾ cup (180ml) skim milk
¼ cup (20g) finely grated parmesan cheese
2kg spinach, trimmed, chopped coarsely
2 cloves garlic, crushed, extra
2 anchovy fillets, drained
2 tablespoons lemon juice
¼ cup (60ml) beef stock

1 Combine mustard, oregano and garlic in small bowl; brush veal both sides with mustard mixture.

2 Cook veal and tomato, in batches, on heated lightly oiled grill plate (or grill or barbecue) until veal is cooked as desired.

3 Meanwhile, bring combined water and salt to a boil in medium saucepan. Add polenta; cook, stirring, about 10 minutes or until polenta thickens. Add milk; cook, stirring, about 5 minutes or until polenta thickens. Stir in cheese.

4 Boil, steam or microwave spinach until just wilted; squeeze out excess liquid with hands. Blend or process spinach with remaining ingredients until smooth.

5 Serve veal chops with tomato, polenta and pureed spinach.

preparation time **15 minutes** cooking time **20 minutes**
serves **4** per serving **7.3g fat; 1626kJ**
tip Fresh rosemary or thyme can be substituted for the oregano.
serving suggestion Top steaks with fresh sage leaves, and serve with a radicchio and rocket salad.

hokkien noodles with beef and snow peas

750g piece beef rump, sliced thinly
¼ cup (60ml) fish sauce
⅓ cup (80ml) oyster sauce
⅓ cup (80ml) sweet chilli sauce
3 cloves garlic, crushed
500g hokkien noodles
2 tablespoons peanut oil
2 large brown onions (400g), sliced thinly
200g snow peas
1 cup (80g) bean sprouts

1 Place beef in large bowl with half the combined sauces and garlic; cover, refrigerate 3 hours or overnight.

2 Place noodles in large heatproof bowl; cover with boiling water, separate with fork, drain.

3 Heat half the oil in wok or large frying pan; stir-fry beef, in batches, until browned.

4 Heat remaining oil in wok; stir-fry onion until soft. Add snow peas and sprouts; stir-fry 1 minute. Return beef and noodles to wok with remaining half of sauce mixture; stir-fry until mixture is hot.

preparation time **15 minutes (plus refrigeration time)**
cooking time **15 minutes**
serves **4** per serving **24.1g fat; 3367kJ**

pepper steak with caramelised onions

1 teaspoon cracked black peppercorns
2 tablespoons finely chopped fresh
   flat-leaf parsley
4 beef sirloin steaks (800g)
¼ cup (60ml) olive oil
2 large brown onions (400g), sliced thinly
2 tablespoons balsamic vinegar
1 tablespoon drained finely chopped
   sun-dried tomatoes in oil
2 cloves garlic, crushed

1 Combine pepper, parsley and beef in large bowl.

2 Heat 1 tablespoon of the oil in large frying pan; cook onion, stirring, about 10 minutes or until browned. Add 1 tablespoon of the vinegar; cook, stirring, 5 minutes or until onions caramelise. Remove from pan; cover to keep warm.

3 Combine remaining oil and vinegar in small screw-top jar with tomato and garlic; shake well.

4 Cook beef on heated oiled grill plate (or grill or barbecue) until cooked as desired. Serve beef with caramelised onions; drizzle with dressing. Serve with mixed salad leaves, if you like.

preparation time **10 minutes** cooking time **15 minutes**
serves **4** per serving **32.2g fat; 2060kJ**

steak with port and pears

425g can pear halves in syrup
⅓ cup (80ml) port
1 clove garlic, crushed
2 teaspoons coarsely chopped fresh chives
1 teaspoon finely grated lemon rind
4 beef eye-fillet steaks (800g)
20g butter
1 tablespoon olive oil
⅓ cup (80ml) beef stock
2 teaspoons cornflour
2 teaspoons water
1 tablespoon coarsely chopped fresh
    chives, extra

1 Drain pears, reserve half a cup syrup. Slice four pear halves thickly. Combine reserved syrup, port, garlic, chives, rind and beef in large bowl, cover; refrigerate 3 hours or overnight.

2 Drain beef; reserve marinade.

3 Heat butter and oil in large frying pan; add beef, cook until browned, Add reserved marinade and stock; bring to a boil. Reduce heat; simmer, covered, about 10 minutes or until beef is cooked. Remove from pan.

4 Strain pan juice, then return juices to pan. Add blended cornflour and the water; stir over heat until sauce boils and thickens. Add sliced pear to pan. [Reserve remaining pear halves for another use.] Stir gently over heat until pear is warmed. Serve beef topped with sauce and pears; sprinkle with extra chives. Serve with steamed vegetables, if you like.

preparation time **15 minutes (plus refrigeration time)**
cooking time **30 minutes**
serves **4** per serving **20.9g fat; 1676 kJ**

satay beef stir-fry

Kecap manis, a thick sweet soy sauce of Indonesian origin, is available at many supermarkets and Asian food stores.

600g hokkien noodles
300g beef rump steak, sliced thinly
½ teaspoon finely grated fresh ginger
2 teaspoons sesame oil
1 small red onion (100g), sliced thinly
1 medium red capsicum (200g), sliced thinly
150g broccoli florets
2 teaspoons lime juice
¼ cup (60ml) satay sauce
1 tablespoon hoisin sauce
⅓ cup (80ml) japanese soy sauce
1 tablespoon kecap manis
150g snow peas
1 tablespoon finely chopped fresh coriander
¼ cup (35g) roasted unsalted peanuts,
  chopped coarsely

1 Place noodles in large heatproof bowl; cover with boiling water, separate with fork, drain.
2 Stir-fry beef and ginger, in batches, in heated oiled wok or large frying pan until browned.
3 Heat oil in same wok; stir-fry onion, capsicum and broccoli until just tender. Return beef to wok with combined juice and sauces; stir-fry until sauce boils. Add noodles and snow peas; stir-fry until hot. Add coriander; stir-fry until combined. Serve sprinkled with nuts.

preparation time **15 minutes** cooking time **15 minutes**
serves **4** per serving **15.8g fat; 2788kJ**
serving suggestion **Serve with a bowl of sambal oelek, the fiery-hot Indonesian chilli and vinegar sauce.**

steak sandwich

Mesclun is a mixture of various baby salad leaves; substitute any single lettuce variety if you prefer. Beef rib-eye is also called scotch fillet by some butchers.

2 small leeks (400g), sliced thinly
1 tablespoon brown sugar
¼ cup (60ml) dry white wine
1 tablespoon wholegrain mustard
2 medium zucchini (240g), sliced thinly
2 baby eggplants (120g), sliced thinly
2 medium tomatoes (300g), sliced thickly
4 x 100g beef rib-eye steaks
8 slices white bread (360g)
50g mesclun

1 Cook leek, with about 2 tablespoons of water to prevent it sticking, in medium frying pan over low heat, stirring, until softened. Add sugar, wine and mustard; cook, stirring, about 10 minutes or until leek is browned and liquid evaporates.

2 Meanwhile, cook zucchini, eggplant and tomato on heated oiled grill plate (or grill or barbecue) until vegetables are just tender. Cover to keep warm.

3 Cook beef on heated oiled grill plate (or grill or barbecue) until cooked as desired.

4 Toast bread lightly. Sandwich each steak, with a quarter each of the vegetables and mesclun, between two pieces of toast.

preparation time **15 minutes** cooking time **15 minutes**
serves **4** per serving **8g fat; 2205kJ**
serving suggestion **Serve with oven-baked potato wedges.**

garlic mustard steak salad

2 cloves garlic, crushed
1kg piece beef rump steak
2 tablespoon olive oil
1 small red onion (100g), sliced thinly
1 medium carrot (120g), cut into matchsticks
1 small green cucumber (130g), seeded,
   cut into matchsticks

dressing
½ cup (125ml) olive oil
¼ cup (60ml) white vinegar
1 tablespoon finely chopped fresh
   flat-leaf parsley
1 tablespoon wholegrain mustard
1 teaspoon caster sugar

1 Rub garlic over beef. Heat oil in large frying pan; cook beef until cooked as desired. Remove from pan; stand, covered, 5 minutes. Slice thinly.
2 Meanwhile, place onion in bowl, cover with boiling water, stand 5 minutes; drain.
3 Make dressing.
3 Combine beef, carrot, cucumber, onion and dressing in large bowl. Serve with crusty bread, if you like.
dressing Combine ingredients in small screw-top jar; shake well.

preparation time **15 minutes** cooking time **10 minutes**
serves **4 per** serving **54.9g fat; 3090kJ**

baked creamy fettuccine with beef

1 tablespoon olive oil
500g beef mince
2 cups (520g) bottled tomato pasta sauce
1 cup (250ml) water
375g fettuccine
200g butter
¾ cup (110g) plain flour
1 litre (4 cups) milk
1¾ cups (220g) coarsely grated
   cheddar cheese
2 cups (140g) stale breadcrumbs
2 tablespoons finely chopped fresh
   flat-leaf parsley

1 Heat oil in large frying pan; cook beef, stirring, until browned. Add pasta sauce and the water; simmer, uncovered, about 15 minutes or until beef mixture thickens.

2 Meanwhile, cook pasta in large saucepan of boiling water, uncovered, until just tender; drain.

3 Melt 150g of the butter in medium saucepan. Add flour; cook, stirring, until mixture boils and thickens. Remove from heat; gradually stir in milk. Return to heat; stir until white sauce boils and thickens. Remove from heat; stir in half the cheese.

4 Melt remaining butter; combine in medium bowl with breadcrumbs, parsley and remaining cheese.

5 Combine pasta with white sauce in shallow 2.5-litre (10-cup) ovenproof dish; top with mince mixture then sprinkle over breadcrumb mixture. [Can be prepared ahead to this point; refrigerate overnight or freeze.]

6 Preheat oven to 180°C/160°C fan-forced.

7 Bake, uncovered, about 30 minutes or until heated through. Serve with greek salad, if you like.

preparation time **10 minutes** cooking time **1 hour**
serves **6** per serving **57.5g fat; 4483kJ**

veal florentine

For an interesting variation, chicken breast fillets can be substituted for the veal.

250g frozen spinach, thawed
1 tablespoon olive oil
8 veal schnitzels (800g)
120g mozzarella cheese, sliced thinly
2⅓ cups (600g) bottled chunky tomato
    pasta sauce
1 tablespoon finely shredded fresh basil

1 Preheat oven to 200°C/180°C fan-forced.
2 Drain spinach then, using hands, squeeze excess liquid from spinach; chop coarsely.
3 Heat oil in large flameproof baking dish; cook veal, in batches, until browned. Return veal to pan, place in single layer; top with spinach, then cheese. Pour combined sauce and basil around veal; bake, uncovered, about 10 minutes or until cheese melts and sauce is hot.

preparation time **5 minutes** cooking time **15 minutes**
serves **4** per serving **16g fat; 1846kJ**

eye-fillet with spicy capsicum relish

You can substitute rib-eye (scotch fillet) or sirloin (New York cut) steak for the eye fillet in this recipe.

3 medium red capsicums (600g)
1 teaspoon olive oil
1 large brown onion (200g), sliced thinly
2 cloves garlic, sliced thinly
2 tablespoons brown sugar
2 tablespoons sherry vinegar
3 fresh small red thai chillies, chopped
    finely
4 beef eye fillet steaks (800g)
2 trimmed corn cobs (500g),
    chopped coarsely
150g sugar snap peas
300g baby new potatoes, halved
2 tablespoons finely chopped fresh
    flat-leaf parsley

1 Quarter capsicums; discard seeds and membranes. Roast under grill or in very hot oven, skin-side up, until skin blisters and blackens. Cover with plastic or paper for 5 minutes; peel away skin, slice thinly.

2 Heat oil in medium frying pan; cook onion and garlic, stirring, until onion is soft. Add sugar, vinegar, chilli and capsicum; cook, stirring, 5 minutes.

3 Meanwhile, cook beef on heated oiled grill plate (or grill or barbecue) until cooked as desired. Remove from heat, stand 5 minutes.

4 Boil, steam or microwave vegetables, separately, until just tender; drain.

5 Top beef with capsicum relish; serve with vegetables, sprinkle with parsley.

preparation time **10 minutes** cooking time **20 minutes**
serves **4** per serving **13g fat; 2327kJ**
tip **You can make the capsicum relish a day ahead; store, covered, in refrigerator. Reheat just before serving.**
serving suggestion **Serve with a green salad with vinaigrette, if you like.**

veal with prosciutto and provolone

30g butter
4 veal leg steaks (320g)
½ cup (125ml) marsala
125g mushrooms, sliced thinly
1 small chicken stock cube, crumbled
2 teaspoons cornflour
2 teaspoons water
4 slices prosciutto (60g)
½ cup (60g) coarsely grated
   provolone cheese

1 Heat butter in large frying pan; add veal, cook until browned. Remove from pan. Add marsala, mushrooms and stock cube to pan; bring to a boil. Reduce heat; simmer, uncovered, 1 minute. Stir in blended cornflour and the water, stir until mixture boils and thickens.

2 Place veal on oven tray, top with prosciutto, spoon over mushroom mixture, sprinkle with cheese. Grill under preheated grill until cheese is melted. Serve veal with pasta and salad, if you like.

preparation time **5 minutes** cooking time **15 minutes**
serves **4** per serving **13g fat; 1545kJ**

beef fillet with nutty couscous

¼ cup (60ml) mild curry paste
750g piece beef fillet
2 medium brown onions (300g),
　chopped finely
2 cups (500ml) beef stock
2 cups (400g) couscous
2 medium (300g) tomatoes, chopped finely
⅓ cup finely chopped fresh mint leaves
⅓ cup (45g) slivered almonds, roasted

1 Rub 1 tablespoon of the curry paste over beef. Cook beef in heated oiled large frying pan, uncovered, until cooked as desired. Remove from pan; cover to keep warm.
2 Add remaining paste and onion to same pan; cook, stirring, until onion is soft. Add stock, bring to a boil; remove from heat. Stir in couscous; stand, covered, 5 minutes.
3 Stir tomato, mint and half the nuts into couscous mixture. Slice beef thinly; serve with couscous, sprinkle with remaining nuts.

preparation time **15 minutes (plus standing time)**
cooking time **15 minutes**
serves **4**　per serving **34g fat; 814kJ**

lemon pepper schnitzel

8 veal schnitzels (800g)
300ml cream
1 teaspoon finely grated lemon rind
2 tablespoons lemon juice
2 teaspoons finely chopped fresh rosemary
1 teaspoon chicken stock powder
1 teaspoon cracked black peppercorns

1 Cook veal in heated oiled large frying pan, in batches, until cooked as desired. Remove from pan; cover to keep warm.

2 Add remaining ingredients to same pan; bring to a boil. Reduce heat; simmer, uncovered, about 5 minutes or until sauce thickens slightly. Return veal to pan; coat with sauce.

preparation time **5 minutes** cooking time **15 minutes**
serves **4** per serving **36.1g fat; 2203kJ**

skewers with chilli-peanut sauce

½ cup (125ml) peanut oil
1 teaspoon sesame oil
¼ cup (35g) roasted unsalted peanuts,
   chopped finely
1 tablespoon honey
2 tablespoons sweet chilli sauce
1 tablespoon lime juice
1kg piece beef rump steak, sliced thinly
2 tablespoons water
1 medium carrot (120g)
2 medium zucchini (240g)

1 Blend or process oils, nuts, honey, sauce and juice until smooth. Thread beef onto 12 skewers; place skewers, in single layer, in shallow dish. Pour peanut sauce over skewers; cover, refrigerate 3 hours or overnight. [Can be prepared ahead to this point; refrigerate for up to 2 days or freeze]

2 Drain skewers; place peanut sauce in small pan with the water, bring to boil. Reduce heat; simmer, stirring, until sauce thickens slightly.

3 Using a vegetable peeler, slice carrot and zucchini into long, thin ribbons.

4 Cook skewers on heated oiled grill plate (or grill or barbecue), in batches, until cooked as desired. Serve drizzled with heated peanut sauce, and carrot and zucchini ribbons.

preparation time **20 minute (plus refrigeration time)**
cooking time **15 minutes**
serves **4** per serving **36.3g fat; 2280kJ**

lamb

moroccan lamb with lemony couscous

Yogurt is used in both the marinade and as the sauce for the lamb in this recipe.

8 lamb fillets (800g)
1 tablespoon ground cumin
1 tablespoon ground coriander
1 teaspoon ground cinnamon
¾ cup (200g) low-fat yogurt
1½ cups (300g) couscous
1½ cups (375ml) boiling water
1 teaspoon peanut oil
⅓ cup (50g) currants
2 teaspoons finely grated lemon rind
2 teaspoons lemon juice
¼ cup coarsely chopped fresh coriander

1 Combine lamb, spices and ⅓ cup of the yogurt in medium bowl, cover; refrigerate 3 hours or overnight.
2 Cook lamb on heated oiled grill plate (or grill or barbecue) until cooked as desired. Cover, stand 5 minutes; slice thinly.
3 Meanwhile, combine couscous, the water and oil in large heatproof bowl, cover; stand 5 minutes or until liquid is absorbed, fluffing with fork occasionally. Stir in currants, rind, juice and fresh coriander.
4 Serve lamb with couscous; drizzle with remaining yogurt.

preparation time **15 minutes (plus refrigeration time)**
cooking time **15 minutes**
serves **4** per serving **9.3g fat; 2193kJ**
tip Substitute some finely chopped preserved lemon for the lemon juice and rind in the couscous, if you like.
serving suggestion Serve with harissa, the fiery North African condiment.

bucatini with spicy lamb sauce

2 teaspoons olive oil
1 small brown onion (80g), chopped finely
2 cloves garlic, crushed
500g lamb mince
1 teaspoon ground cumin
½ teaspoon ground cayenne pepper
½ teaspoon ground cinnamon
2 tablespoons tomato paste
2 x 415g cans crushed tomatoes
1 large green zucchini (150g),
    chopped coarsely
2 tablespoons finely chopped fresh mint
375g bucatini

1   Heat oil in large saucepan; cook onion and garlic, stirring, until onion softens. Add lamb; cook, stirring, until changed in colour. Add spices; cook, stirring, until fragrant.
2   Stir in paste, undrained tomatoes and zucchini; bring to a boil. Reduce heat; simmer, uncovered, about 15 minutes or until sauce thickens slightly. Stir in mint.
3   Meanwhile, cook pasta in large saucepan of boiling water, uncovered, until just tender; drain. Serve pasta topped with sauce.

preparation time **10 minutes** cooking time **20 minutes**
serves **4** per serving **11.9g fat; 2357kJ**

lamb and pasta with walnut pesto

You need approximately two bunches of fresh coriander for this recipe, including the roots and stems as well as the leaves.

375g bow tie pasta
4 lamb fillets (400g)
1½ cups coarsely chopped fresh coriander
½ cup (50g) walnuts, roasted
½ cup (40g) coarsely grated
    parmesan cheese
2 cloves garlic, quartered
½ cup (125ml) olive oil
1 tablespoon drained preserved lemons,
    chopped finely
½ cup (140g) yogurt
2 teaspoons olive oil, extra
2 teaspoons lemon juice

1 Cook pasta in large saucepan of boiling water, uncovered, until just tender; drain. Rinse under cold water; drain.
2 Meanwhile, cook lamb in large frying pan until cooked as desired. Stand 5 minutes; slice thinly.
3 Reserve 2 tablespoons of coriander leaves. Blend or process nuts, remaining coriander, cheese, garlic and oil until mixture forms a smooth paste. Combine pesto with pasta in large bowl.
4 Divide pasta mixture among serving plates, top with lamb and lemon; drizzle salad with combined yogurt, oil and juice, top with reserved coriander leaves.

preparation time **10 minutes** cooking time **15 minutes**
serves **4** per serving **48.5g fat; 3628kJ**

lamb and vegetable soup

1 tablespoon olive oil
4 lamb shanks (1kg)
1 large brown onion (200g),
  chopped coarsely
2 trimmed celery stalks (200g), sliced thinly
2 small carrots (140g), chopped coarsely
1 medium parsnip (125g), chopped coarsely
1 medium swede (225g), chopped coarsely
1 medium potato (200g), chopped coarsely
2 x 410g cans crushed tomatoes
2 tablespoons worcestershire sauce
2 litres (8 cups) water

1 Heat oil in large saucepan; cook lamb shanks, uncovered, until browned. Remove from pan. Place onion, celery, carrot, parsnip, swede and potato in same pan; cook, stirring, until onion is soft.
2 Return shanks to pan with undrained tomatoes, sauce and the water; bring to a boil. Reduce heat; simmer, covered, 2 hours, stirring occasionally. Cool; refrigerate overnight.
3 Remove and discard fat from soup. Remove shanks; cut meat from bones, discard bones. Chop meat coarsely; return meat to soup. [Can be prepared ahead to this point; refrigerate for up to 2 days or freeze]
4 Bring soup to a boil. Reduce heat; simmer, uncovered, about 15 minutes or until heated through.

preparation time **20 minutes (plus refrigeration time)**
cooking time **2 hours 40 minutes**
serves **4** per serving **12.8g fat; 1531kJ**

balinese lamb chops

1 tablespoon peanut oil
12 lamb loin chops (1.2kg), trimmed
2 small brown onions (1760g), sliced thinly
½ cup (130g) crunchy peanut butter
¼ cup (60ml) sweet chilli sauce
2 tablespoons lemon juice
⅔ cup (160ml) coconut milk
½ cup (125ml) water
1 tablespoon finely chopped fresh coriander

1   Heat oil in large frying pan; cook lamb, uncovered, until cooked as desired. Remove from pan; cover to keep warm.
2   Drain excess fat from pan. Add onion; cook, stirring, until browned. Add peanut butter, sauce, juice and combined coconut milk and the water to pan; cook, stirring, until sauce thickens slightly. Stir in coriander; return lamb to pan, coat with sauce.

preparation time **10 minutes** cooking time **20 minutes**
serves 6 per serving **32.9g fat; 2019kJ**

lamb with mango chutney and rocket salad

⅓ cup (95g) yogurt
⅓ cup (110g) mango chutney
⅓ cup (80ml) mild chilli sauce
12 french-trimmed lamb cutlets (600g)
250g sugar snap peas
150g rocket, trimmed
¼ cup (60ml) olive oil
2 tablespoons balsamic vinegar

1 Combine yogurt, chutney and sauce in large bowl.
2 Cook lamb on heated grill plate (or grill or barbecue), brushing frequently with yogurt mixture, until cooked as desired.
3 Meanwhile, boil, steam or microwave peas until just tender. Rinse peas under cold water; drain. Combine peas and rocket in large bowl with combined oil and vinegar. Serve rocket salad with lamb.

preparation time **10 minutes** cooking time **10 minutes**
serves **4** per serving **28.3g fat; 1755kJ**

rosemary lamb open sandwich

4 lamb fillets (400g)
2 cloves garlic, crushed
¼ cup (60ml) lemon juice
2 tablespoons fresh rosemary leaves
1 tablespoon wholegrain mustard
2 small tomatoes (180g)
170g asparagus, halved crossways
4 slices light rye bread (180g)
100g butter lettuce, chopped coarsely

1 Combine lamb, garlic, juice, rosemary and mustard in large bowl, cover; refrigerate 3 hours or overnight.
2 Cut each tomato into six wedges. Cook tomato and asparagus, in batches, on heated oiled grill plate (or grill or barbecue) until browned lightly and just tender. Toast bread both sides.
3 Drain lamb; discard marinade. Cook lamb on same heated grill plate (or grill or barbecue) until cooked as desired. Cover, stand 5 minutes; slice thickly.
4 Place one slice of the toast on each serving plate; top each slice with equal amounts of lettuce, tomato, asparagus and lamb.

preparation time **5 minutes (plus refrigeration time)**
cooking time **15 minutes**
serves **4** per serving **4.8g fat; 1042kJ**
tip **Substitute toasted sourdough or ciabatta for the rye bread, if you like.**

farfalle with lamb, rocket and herbs

This salad can be served warm or cold. You can substitute your favourite pasta for the farfalle.

375g farfalle pasta
250g yellow teardrop tomatoes, halved
1 medium red onion (170g), sliced thinly
50g baby rocket leaves
¼ cup finely shredded fresh basil
1 tablespoon fresh thyme leaves
400g lamb fillets
2 cloves garlic, crushed
1 tablespoon wholegrain mustard
¼ cup (60ml) balsamic vinegar

1 Cook pasta in large saucepan of boiling water, uncovered, until just tender; drain.
2 Combine tomato, onion, rocket, basil and thyme in large bowl.
3 Rub lamb with combined garlic and mustard; cook on heated oiled grill plate (or grill or barbecue) until cooked as desired. Cover, stand 5 minutes; slice thinly.
4 Add pasta, lamb and vinegar to tomato mixture; toss to combine.

preparation time **20 minutes**
cooking time **10 minutes (plus standing time)**
serves **4** per serving **4.9g fat; 1910kJ**

lamb chermoulla with chickpea salad

Chermoulla is a Moroccan mixture of fresh and ground spices including coriander, cumin and paprika. It can be used as a marinade for chicken, meat and fish.

300g green beans, trimmed
2 teaspoons cracked black peppercorns
2 teaspoons ground cumin
2 teaspoons ground coriander
1 teaspoon hot paprika
2 tablespoons coarsely chopped fresh
    flat-leaf parsley
2 tablespoons coarsely chopped fresh
    coriander leaves
2 tablespoons coarsely chopped fresh
    mint leaves
1 tablespoon coarsely grated lemon rind
¼ cup (60ml) water
1 medium red onion (170g), chopped finely
8 lamb fillets (700g)
400g can brown lentils, rinsed, drained
300g can chickpeas, rinsed, drained
⅓ cup coarsely chopped fresh flat-leaf
    parsley, extra
2 cloves garlic, crushed
2 tablespoons lemon juice

1 Cut beans into 3cm lengths; boil, steam or microwave beans until just tender. Rinse under cold water; drain.

2 Blend or process pepper, spices, herbs, rind, the water and half the onion until mixture forms a smooth paste.

3 Combine lamb with chermoulla paste in large bowl; cook, in batches, on heated oiled grill plate (or grill or barbecue) until cooked as desired. Cover, stand 5 minutes; slice thickly.

4 Combine beans, lentils, chickpeas, extra parsley, garlic and juice with remaining onion in large bowl. Serve chickpea salad with lamb.

preparation time **15 minutes** cooking time **15 minutes**
serves **4** per serving **8.3g fat; 1373kJ**
tip **The salad can be assembled several hours ahead; add juice just before serving.**
serving suggestion **Serve with a bowl of minted yogurt.**

minted lamb skewers

1kg lamb fillets
1 tablespoon mild curry powder
1 tablespoon finely chopped fresh
   lemon grass
2 teaspoons grated fresh ginger
¼ cup (60ml) peanut oil
½ cup finely chopped fresh mint leaves
1 tablespoon fish sauce
4 cloves garlic, crushed
1 cup (150g) pistachios, chopped finely

1 Cut lamb into 2cm cubes. Combine curry powder, lemon grass, ginger, oil, mint, sauce and garlic in large bowl; add lamb, coat with spice mixture.

2 Thread lamb onto 12 skewers. Place skewers in shallow large dish. Cover; refrigerate 3 hours or overnight. [Can be prepared ahead to this point; refrigerate for up to 2 days or freeze]

3 Place nuts on oven tray; roll skewers in nuts. Cook skewers on heated oiled grill plate (or grill or barbecue) until cooked as desired.

preparation time **20 minutes (plus refrigeration time)**
cooking time **10 minutes**
serves **4** per serving **42g fat; 2726kJ**

lamb shanks with barley in red wine

8 french-trimmed lamb shanks (2kg)
2 medium brown onions (300g),
    cut into thick wedges
3 cloves garlic, crushed
4 medium carrots (480g), chopped finely
½ cup (65g) pearl barley, rinsed
1 cup (250ml) dry red wine
1 cup (250ml) beef stock
410g can crushed tomatoes
¼ cup (60ml) tomato paste
1 tablespoon finely chopped fresh thyme

1 Cook lamb, in batches, in heated oiled large saucepan until browned lightly. Add onion and garlic to same pan; cook, stirring, until onion is soft.
2 Return lamb to pan; add carrot, barley, wine, stock, undrained tomatoes and paste, bring to boil. Reduce heat; simmer, covered, 1¾ hours, stirring occasionally. [Can be prepared ahead to this point; refrigerate overnight or freeze]
3 Stir in thyme; simmer, uncovered, about 15 minutes or until lamb is tender.

preparation time **10 minutes**
cooking time **2 hours 20 minutes**
serves **4** per serving **25.5g fat; 2655kJ**

lamb with blueberry mint sauce

425g can blueberries in syrup
15g butter
600g lamb fillet
1 clove garlic, crushed
2 rindless bacon rashers (130g),
    chopped finely
½ cup (125ml) water
2 teaspoons lemon juice
1 tablespoon finely chopped fresh mint
2 teaspoons cornflour
2 teaspoons water, extra

1 Drain blueberries, reserve half the blueberries and quarter cup of the syrup. [Remaining blueberries and syrup are not used in this recipe]

2 Heat butter in large frying pan; cook lamb until browned. Remove lamb from pan.

3 Discard all but 1 tablespoon of pan juices, add garlic and bacon to pan, cook, stirring, until bacon is crisp. Add reserved blueberry syrup, water, lemon juice and mint to pan; bring to a boil. Reduce heat; simmer, uncovered, 2 minutes.

4 Stir in blended cornflour and the extra water, stir over heat until mixture boils and thickens. Add reserved blueberries, stir over heat until heated through. Slice lamb thickly; serve drizzled with blueberry sauce, and steamed vegetables, if you like.

preparation time **10 minutes** cooking time **30 minutes**
serves **4** per serving **12.9g fat; 1383kJ**

lamb cutlets with endive salad and croutons

Crouton comes from the French word croûte, which translates as crust – hence these crunchy pieces of garlic bread that soak up the sauce in this dish.

4 slices white bread (180g)
1 tablespoon vegetable oil
1 clove garlic, crushed
4 medium zucchini (480g), sliced thinly
4 baby eggplants (240g), sliced thinly
8 french-trimmed lamb cutlets (600g)
½ cup (125ml) balsamic vinegar
½ cup (125ml) beef stock
150g curly endive, trimmed
3 medium tomatoes (450g),
   chopped coarsely
¼ cup coarsely chopped fresh
   flat-leaf parsley

1 Preheat oven to 220°C/200°C.
2 Trim crusts from bread; discard crusts. Halve each slice diagonally; combine with oil and garlic in small bowl. Place bread, in single layer, on oven tray; bake, uncovered, turning once, about 4 minutes each side or until browned lightly and crisp.
3 Cook zucchini and eggplant in heated large frying pan until just tender; cover to keep warm. Cook lamb, in batches, in same pan until cooked as desired; cover to keep warm.
4 Place vinegar in same pan; bring to a boil. Add stock; reduce heat. Simmer, uncovered, until sauce reduces by half.
5 Serve lamb on croutons with combined zucchini, eggplant, endive, tomato and parsley. Drizzle with balsamic dressing.

preparation time **10 minutes** cooking time **15 minutes**
serves **4** per serving **15.1g fat; 1372kJ**
tip **Croutons can be made a day ahead and stored in an airtight container.**

penne with lamb and roasted capsicum

3 large red capsicums (1kg)
500g lamb fillets
2 tablespoons olive oil
2 teaspoons ground cumin
2 x 415g cans tomato puree
½ cup (60g) drained semi-dried tomatoes
   in oil, chopped coarsely
375g penne
¼ cup finely shredded fresh basil

1 Quarter capsicums; discard seeds and membranes. Roast under heated grill or in very hot oven, skin-side up, until skin blisters and blackens. Cover capsicum pieces with plastic or paper for 5 minutes; peel away skin, then slice thinly.

2 Combine lamb, oil and cumin in medium bowl. Cook lamb, in batches, in heated large oiled frying pan (or grill or barbecue) until cooked as desired. Cover, stand 5 minutes; slice thinly.

3 Heat large frying pan; add puree, tomato and capsicum; bring to a boil. Reduce heat; simmer, uncovered, about 5 minutes or until sauce thickens slightly.

4 Meanwhile, cook pasta in large saucepan of boiling water, uncovered, until just tender; drain. Combine pasta in large bowl with lamb, tomato sauce and basil.

preparation time **10 minutes** cooking time **15 minutes**
serves **4** per serving 12.8g fat; 2747kJ

lamb with avocado and red onion salsa

3 cloves garlic, crushed
1 tablespoon balsamic vinegar
¼ cup (60ml) lemon juice
2 tablespoons olive oil
12 french-trimmed lamb cutlets (600g)
1 large avocado (320g), chopped coarsely
1 medium red onion (170g), chopped finely
1 tablespoon finely chopped fresh coriander

1 Combine garlic, vinegar, 1 tablespoon of the juice, 2 teaspoons of the oil and lamb in large bowl. Cover; refrigerate 10 minutes.
2 Meanwhile, combine remaining juice and remaining oil in small bowl with avocado, onion and coriander.
3 Cook lamb on heated grill plate (or grill or barbecue) until cooked as desired; serve with salsa.

preparation time **15 minutes (plus refrigeration time)**
cooking time **10 minutes**
serves **4** per serving **16.7g fat; 798kJ**

tandoori lamb with cucumber raita

8 lamb fillets (800g)
1 tablespoon tandoori paste
1½ cups (400g) low-fat yogurt
1 lebanese cucumber (130g), seeded,
    chopped finely
2 green onions, chopped finely
½ teaspoon ground cumin
1 teaspoon ground cardamom
2 cups (400g) basmati rice
pinch saffron threads

1 Combine lamb with paste and half of the yogurt in large bowl. Combine remaining yogurt in small bowl with cucumber, onion and half of the combined spices.
2 Place rice and saffron in large saucepan of boiling water; cook, uncovered, until rice is tender. Drain rice; place in large bowl.
3 Cook remaining spices in heated small frying pan until fragrant; stir into saffron rice, cover to keep warm.
4 Cook undrained lamb, in batches, on heated lightly oiled grill plate (or grill or barbecue) until cooked as desired.
5 Serve lamb on saffron rice, topped with cucumber raita.

preparation time **10 minutes** cooking time **20 minutes**
serves **4** per serving **38.1g fat; 3727kJ**
tip **You can marinate the lamb a day ahead; store, covered, in refrigerator. Similarly, the cucumber raita can be made several hours ahead; store, covered, in refrigerator.**
serving suggestion **Serve with a fresh tomato and onion sambal, and pappadums.**

combination fried rice

1½ cups (300g) white long-grain rice
200g pork sausages
2 tablespoons peanut oil
2 eggs, beaten lightly
230g baby corn, chopped coarsely
1 medium red capsicum (200g), sliced thinly
1 cup (80g) bean sprouts
6 green onions, chopped coarsely
1 tablespoon japanese soy sauce
1 tablespoon oyster sauce

1   Cook rice in large saucepan of boiling water, uncovered, until just tender; drain.
2   Meanwhile, cook sausages, uncovered, in heated oiled large frying pan until cooked through; drain on absorbent paper. Slice sausages thinly; combine with rice in large bowl. [Can be prepared ahead to this point; refrigerate overnight or freeze]
3   Heat 1 teaspoon of the oil in wok or large pan; cook egg, tilting pan, over medium heat until omelette is almost set. Roll omelette; cut into thin strips.
4   Heat remaining oil in same wok; stir-fry corn, capsicum, sprouts and onion until vegetables are just tender. Add rice mixture, omelette and combined sauces; stir-fry until hot.

preparation time **15 minutes** cooking time **20 minutes**
serves **4** per serving **25.4g fat; 2593kJ**

orecchiette with ham, artichokes and sun-dried tomatoes

375g orecchiette pasta
500g leg ham, chopped coarsely
340g jar artichoke hearts in oil,
    drained, quartered
½ cup (75g) sun-dried tomatoes, halved
1 cup (80g) flaked parmesan cheese
1 cup loosely packed fresh flat-leaf parsley
2 tablespoons lemon juice
1 tablespoon wholegrain mustard
1 tablespoon honey
1 clove garlic, crushed
½ cup (125ml) olive oil

1   Cook pasta in large saucepan of boiling water, uncovered, until just tender; drain.
2   Place pasta in large bowl with ham, artichoke, tomato, cheese, parsley and combined remaining ingredients; toss gently to combine.

preparation time **10 minutes** cooking time **15 minutes**
serves **4** per serving **46.1g fat; 3771kJ**

linguine with creamy mushroom and chorizo sauce

300g swiss brown mushrooms, halved
2 tablespoons olive oil
2 cloves garlic, crushed
2 chorizo sausages (340g)
½ cup (125ml) dry white wine
1 cup (250ml) chicken stock
300g sour cream
4 green onions, chopped finely
375g linguine
2 tablespoons finely shredded fresh basil

1 Preheat oven to 240°C/220°C fan-forced.
2 Place mushroom in shallow large baking dish, drizzle with combined oil and garlic; roast, uncovered, 15 minutes.
3 Meanwhile, cook chorizo in heated medium frying pan until browned and cooked through; drain on absorbent paper, slice thinly.
4 Bring wine to a boil in same cleaned pan. Reduce heat; simmer, uncovered, 5 minutes. Stir in stock and cream; return to a boil. Reduce heat; simmer, uncovered, about 2 minutes or until sauce is hot. Remove sauce from heat; stir in mushroom and onion.
5 Meanwhile, cook pasta in large saucepan of boiling water, uncovered, until just tender; drain. Combine pasta in large bowl with mushroom sauce, chorizo and basil.

preparation time **10 minutes** cooking time **20 minutes**
serves **4** per serving **65.6g fat; 4305kJ**

roasted potato, bacon and egg salad

750g baby new potatoes, halved
½ cup (125ml) olive oil
6 eggs
4 rindless bacon rashers (260g),
    chopped coarsely
200g baby spinach leaves
2 tablespoons white wine vinegar
4 anchovy fillets, drained
2 tablespoons coarsely grated
    parmesan cheese

1 Preheat oven to 240°C/220°C fan-forced.
2 Combine potato and 2 tablespoons of the oil in large baking dish; bake, uncovered, 25 minutes.
3 Meanwhile, cover eggs with water in medium pan; bring to boil. Reduce heat; simmer, uncovered, 10 minutes; drain. Rinse eggs under cold water; peel and quarter.
3 Cook bacon in heated large frying pan until crisp; drain on absorbent paper. Combine bacon in large bowl with potato, egg, spinach and processed vinegar, anchovy and cheese.

preparation time **10 minutes** cooking time **30 minutes**
serves **4** per serving **48g fat; 2828kJ**

chilli, chutney and coconut pork

750g pork strips
1 cup (320g) mango chutney
2 fresh small red thai chillies,
    chopped finely
1 tablespoon ground cumin
2 cloves garlic, crushed
2 teaspoons grated fresh ginger
2 tablespoons lemon juice
1 large red capsicum (350g), sliced thinly
1 cup (250ml) coconut milk
½ cup coarsely chopped fresh coriander

1   Combine pork, chutney, chilli, cumin, garlic, ginger and juice in large bowl. Cover; refrigerate 3 hours or overnight. [Can be prepared ahead to this point; refrigerate overnight or freeze]

2   Cook capsicum in heated oiled wok or large frying pan, stirring, until almost soft; remove from pan.

3   Stir-fry pork mixture, in batches, in same pan until pork is cooked. Add capsicum and milk; cook, stirring, about 1 minute or until hot. Just before serving, stir in coriander.

preparation time **10 minutes (plus refrigeration time)**
cooking time **15 minutes**
serves **4** per serving **17.7g fat; 2127kJ**

pork, kumara and lentil curry

750g piece pork neck
2 medium brown onions (300g), sliced thinly
¼ cup (75g) mild curry paste
2 x 410g cans crushed tomatoes
1 large kumara (500g), chopped coarsely
½ cup (100g) red lentils
1 cup (250ml) coconut milk
500g spinach, trimmed, chopped coarsely
1 tablespoon finely chopped fresh coriander

1 Cut pork into 2cm cubes; cook in heated oiled large frying pan, in batches, until well browned. Add onion and paste to same pan; cook, uncovered, until onion is soft.

2 Return pork to pan, stir in undrained tomatoes; bring to a boil. Reduce heat; simmer, covered, 1¼ hours. [Can be prepared ahead to this point; refrigerate overnight or freeze]

3 Meanwhile, cook kumara, uncovered, in heated oiled medium frying pan until just browned. Add kumara to pork mixture, stir in lentils; bring to a boil. Reduce heat; simmer, uncovered, about 15 minutes or until kumara and lentils are tender.

4 Stir in milk, spinach and coriander; cook, stirring until spinach is just wilted.

preparation time **15 minutes** cooking time **2 hours**
serves **4** per serving **35.2g fat; 3039kJ**

madras pork curry

1 tablespoon peanut oil
750g pork strips
1 large brown onion (200g), sliced thickly
¼ cup (75g) madras curry paste
1 cup (250ml) coconut milk
2 tablespoons finely chopped fresh mint
¼ cup finely chopped fresh coriander
2 large tomatoes (440g), seeded,
   sliced thickly

1   Heat oil in large frying pan; cook pork, in batches, until browned.
2   Add onion to same pan; cook, stirring, until browned lightly. Stir in paste; cook, uncovered, until fragrant.
3   Return pork to pan with milk, mint, coriander and tomato; bring to a boil. Reduce heat; simmer, uncovered, about 10 minutes, or until curry sauce thickens slightly and mixture is hot.

preparation time **10 minutes** cooking time **25 minutes**
serves **4** per serving **27.8g fat; 1988kJ**

pork fillet with apple and leek

Pork has a natural affinity with both apple and onion; here, these traditional accompaniments are given a contemporary twist.

800g pork fillets
¾ cup (180ml) chicken stock
2 medium leeks (700g), sliced thickly
1 clove garlic, crushed
2 tablespoons brown sugar
2 tablespoons red wine vinegar
2 medium apples (300g)
10g butter
1 tablespoon brown sugar, extra
400g baby carrots, trimmed,
   halved lengthways
8 medium patty-pan squash (240g),
   quartered
250g asparagus, trimmed, chopped coarsely

1 Preheat oven to 240°C/220°C fan-forced.
2 Place pork, in single layer, in large baking dish; roast, uncovered, about 25 minutes or until cooked as desired. Cover, stand 5 minutes; slice thickly.
3 Meanwhile, heat half the stock in medium frying pan; cook leek and garlic, stirring, until leek is soft. Add sugar and vinegar; cook, stirring, about 5 minutes or until leek caramelises. Add remaining stock; bring to a boil. Reduce heat; simmer, uncovered, about 5 minutes or until liquid reduces by half. Place leek mixture in medium bowl; cover to keep warm.
4 Peel, core and halve apples; slice thickly.
5 Melt butter in same pan; cook apple and extra sugar, stirring, until apple is browned and tender.
6 Boil, steam or microwave carrot, squash and asparagus, separately, until just tender; drain.
7 Serve pork and vegetables topped with caramelised apple and leek.

preparation time **10 minutes** cooking time **25 minutes**
serves **4** per serving **7.5g fat; 1624kJ**

thai stir-fried pork

750g pork strips
¼ cup (75g) green curry paste
115g fresh baby corn, halved lengthways
1 large red capsicum (350g), sliced thinly
⅔ cup (160ml) coconut milk
1½ tablespoons lime juice
200g baby spinach leaves
⅓ cup coarsely shredded fresh basil

1 Cook pork, in batches, in heated oiled wok or large frying pan until browned. Cover to keep warm.
2 Cook paste in wok, stirring, until fragrant. Add corn and capsicum; stir-fry 2 minutes. Add milk and juice; stir-fry 2 minutes. Return pork to pan with spinach and basil; stir-fry until leaves just wilt.

preparation time **5 minutes** cooking time **15 minutes**
serves **4** per serving **19.1g fat; 1735kJ**

steamed pork rice-paper rolls

When soaked in hot water, Vietnamese rice-paper sheets (banh trang) make pliable wrappers for a host of fillings. You will need a small chinese cabbage for this recipe.

350g pork mince
1 clove garlic, crushed
1 teaspoon grated fresh ginger
1 teaspoon five-spice powder
4¼ cups (340g) finely shredded
   chinese cabbage
4 green onions, sliced thinly
1 tablespoon japanese soy sauce
¼ cup (60ml) oyster sauce
¼ cup coarsely chopped fresh coriander
12 x 22cm rice paper sheets
¼ cup (60ml) sweet chilli sauce
2 tablespoons lime juice

1 Cook pork, garlic, ginger and spice in large frying pan, stirring, until pork is browned.
2 Add cabbage, onion, soy sauce, oyster sauce and 2 tablespoons of the coriander to pan; cook, stirring, until cabbage is just wilted.
3 Place one sheet of rice paper in medium bowl of warm water until softened slightly; lift sheet carefully from water, place on board, pat dry with absorbent paper. Place a twelfth of the filling mixture in centre of sheet; fold in sides, roll top to bottom to enclose filling. Repeat with remaining rice paper sheets and filling.
4 Place rolls, in single layer, in large baking-paper-lined bamboo steamer set over large saucepan of simmering water; steam, covered, about 5 minutes or until hot. Serve rolls with dipping sauce made with combined remaining coriander, chilli sauce and juice.

preparation time **30 minutes** cooking time **5 minutes** serves **4** per serving **7.5g fat; 982kJ**
tip **Rolls can be prepared a day ahead; store, covered, in refrigerator.**

pork with ratatouille

In a Provençale dialect, touiller means to stir and crush, thus the name ratatouille perfectly describes this rich vegetable stew.

1kg baby new potatoes, halved
1 medium brown onion (150g),
    chopped coarsely
2 cloves garlic, crushed
4 baby eggplants (240g), chopped coarsely
2 medium green zucchini (240g),
    chopped coarsely
410g can crushed tomatoes
2 tablespoons finely shredded fresh basil
4 pork steaks (600g)

1   Preheat oven to 240°C/220°C fan-forced.
2   Place potato in lightly oiled large baking dish; roast, uncovered, about 25 minutes or until browned and crisp.
3   Meanwhile, cook onion and garlic in heated large frying pan, stirring, until onion is soft. Stir in eggplant and zucchini; cook, stirring, until vegetables are just tender.
4   Stir in undrained tomatoes; bring to a boil. Reduce heat; simmer, uncovered, about 5 minutes or until vegetables are tender and sauce thickens. Stir in basil.
5   Cook pork, in batches, in heated oiled medium frying pan until cooked as desired. Slice thickly.
6   Serve pork with potatoes and ratatouille.

preparation time **10 minutes** cooking time **25 minutes**
serves **4** per serving **6.2g fat; 1652kJ**
tip Ratatouille can be made a day ahead; store, covered, in refrigerator.

pork valenciana

4 pork loin chops (1.1kg)
½ cup (175g) orange marmalade
2 tablespoons mild chilli sauce
1 tablespoon cider vinegar
1 teaspoon grated fresh ginger
1 teaspoon ground cumin
3 green onions, sliced thinly

1 Cook pork, uncovered, in heated large oiled pan until cooked as desired. Remove from pan; cover to keep warm.
2 Meanwhile, cook marmalade, sauce, vinegar, ginger and cumin in small pan, stirring, until sauce thickens slightly; stir in onion. Serve pork drizzled with sauce, and accompanied with steamed buk choy, if you like.

preparation time **5 minutes** cooking time **10 minutes**
serves **4** per serving **19.5g fat; 1819kJ**

spinach and prosciutto salad

375g large pasta spirals
12 slices prosciutto (180g)
150g baby spinach leaves
2 tablespoons wholegrain mustard
2 cloves garlic, crushed
½ cup (125ml) olive oil
¼ cup (60ml) lemon juice

1 Cook pasta in large saucepan of boiling water, uncovered, until tender; drain. Rinse under cold water; drain.
2 Meanwhile, cook prosciutto, in batches, in heated large frying pan until browned and crisp; drain on absorbent paper, chop coarsely.
3 Place pasta and prosciutto in large bowl with spinach and combined remaining ingredients; toss gently to combine.

preparation time **10 minutes** cooking time **10 minutes**
serves **4** per serving **32.4g fat; 2688kJ**
tip Finely slice two hard-boiled eggs and toss them through the salad just before serving, if you like.

meatballs with chilli mushroom sauce

250g pork mince
250g veal mince
1 cup (70g) stale breadcrumbs
¼ cup finely chopped fresh oregano
3 cloves garlic, crushed
⅓ cup (95g) tomato paste
1 egg, beaten lightly
1 tablespoon olive oil
250g button mushrooms, sliced thinly
2 x 410g cans crushed tomatoes
¼ cup (60ml) mild chilli sauce

1 Preheat oven to 200°C/180°C fan-forced.
2 Combine mince, breadcrumbs, oregano, garlic, paste and egg in medium bowl; roll level tablespoons of mixture into balls. Place meatballs on oiled oven tray; cook, uncovered, about 15 minutes or until cooked.
3 Meanwhile, heat oil in large saucepan; cook mushrooms, stirring, until just soft. Add undrained tomatoes and sauce to pan; bring to a boil. Reduce heat; simmer, uncovered, 5 minutes. Add meatballs; cook, stirring, 2 minutes.

preparation time **15 minutes** cooking time **20 minutes** serves **4** per serving **12g fat; 1276kJ**

vegetables

gnocchi with herb and mushroom sauce

Gnocchi are small dumplings made of such ingredients as flour, potatoes, semolina, ricotta cheese or spinach. They make a great base for a full-flavoured sauce such as this, packed with herbs, red wine and mushrooms.

1 tablespoon vegetable oil
1 medium brown onion (150g),
   chopped coarsely
2 cloves garlic, crushed
400g swiss brown mushrooms, sliced thinly
1 tablespoon plain flour
⅓ cup (80ml) dry red wine
2 teaspoons japanese soy sauce
⅔ cup (160ml) vegetable stock
1 tablespoon light sour cream
1 tablespoon coarsely chopped
   fresh oregano
1 tablespoon finely chopped fresh sage
600g potato gnocchi

1 Heat oil in large frying pan; cook onion, garlic and mushrooms, stirring, until onion is soft. Add flour; cook, stirring, 1 minute.
2 Add wine, sauce, stock and cream; cook, stirring, until sauce thickens slightly. Stir in herbs.
3 Meanwhile, cook gnocchi in large saucepan of boiling water, uncovered, until gnocchi rise to the surface and are just tender; drain. Add gnocchi to herb and mushroom sauce; toss gently to combine.

preparation time **10 minutes** cooking time **15 minutes**
serves **4** per serving **7.6g fat; 1397kJ**
tip You could substitute button or oyster mushrooms for the swiss brown mushrooms.
serving suggestion Serve with a green salad, dressed with herb vinaigrette, and fresh crusty bread.

pea and potato soup

Leek and potato are natural allies when teamed in a satisfying winter soup. Take care to wash the leeks well under cold water to remove any grit.

3 cups (750ml) chicken stock
2 medium leeks (700g), sliced thinly
1 clove garlic, crushed
2 medium potatoes (400g), chopped coarsely
4 cups (500g) frozen peas
3 cups (750ml) water
2 tablespoons finely shredded fresh mint

1 Heat 2 tablespoons of the stock in large saucepan, add leek and garlic; cook, stirring, about 10 minutes or until leek is soft.
2 Add remaining stock, potato, peas and the water to pan; bring to a boil. Reduce heat; simmer, covered, about 15 minutes or until vegetables are tender. Cool 10 minutes.
3 Blend or process cooled soup, in batches, until smooth.
4 Return soup to same cleaned pan; stir over heat until hot. Stir in mint just before serving.

preparation time **10 minutes**
cooking time **30 minutes (plus cooling time)**
serves **4** per serving **1.8g fat; 822kJ**
serving suggestion **Herb scones or damper would make a good accompaniment for this soup.**

tomato, fetta and spinach galettes

There are many different bottled pestos on supermarket shelves these days; we chose a pesto flavoured with sun-dried tomatoes.

250g frozen spinach, thawed
2 sheets ready-rolled puff pastry
⅓ cup (80ml) bottled pesto
200g soft fetta cheese, crumbled
¼ cup finely chopped fresh basil
250g cherry tomatoes, halved
¼ cup (20g) coarsely grated
   parmesan cheese
1 teaspoon cracked black peppercorns

1 Preheat oven to 240°C/220°C fan-forced.
2 Drain spinach then, using hands, squeeze excess liquid from spinach; chop coarsely.
3 Oil two oven trays; place 1 sheet of pastry on each. Fold edges of pastry inward to form 1cm border. Divide pesto between bases; spread evenly to cover base. Top each with spinach, fetta, basil and tomato; sprinkle with parmesan and pepper. Cook, uncovered, about 15 minutes or until crisp and browned lightly.

preparation time **20 minutes** cooking time **15 minutes**
serves **6** per serving **41.4g fat; 2445kJ**

grilled haloumi, tomato and eggplant salad

½ cup (125ml) olive oil
4 baby eggplants (240g), sliced
  thinly lengthways
4 medium egg tomatoes (300g),
  halved lengthways
400g haloumi cheese, sliced thinly
250g rocket, trimmed, chopped coarsely
¼ cup firmly packed fresh basil leaves
2 tablespoons red wine vinegar
2 teaspoons coarsely chopped
  drained capers

1 Heat 1 tablespoon of the oil in large frying pan; cook eggplant until browned both sides. Remove from pan.
2 Add tomato to same pan; cook, cut-side down, until browned and softened slightly. Remove from pan.
3 Heat another tablespoon of the oil in same pan; cook cheese until browned lightly both sides.
4 Combine eggplant, tomato, haloumi, rocket and basil in large bowl with remaining oil, vinegar and capers.

preparation time **15 minutes** cooking time **15 minutes**
serves **4** per serving **46.2g fat; 2275kJ**

chickpea and pumpkin curry

In Indian cooking, the word masala loosely translates as paste; the word tikka refers to a bite-sized piece of meat, poultry, fish or vegetable. A jar labelled tikka masala contains spices and oils, mixed to a mild paste.

2 teaspoons peanut oil
2 medium brown onions (300g), sliced thinly
2 cloves garlic, crushed
2 tablespoons tikka masala curry paste
2 cups (500ml) vegetable stock
1 cup (250ml) water
1kg butternut pumpkin, chopped coarsely
2 cups (400g) jasmine rice
300g can chickpeas, rinsed, drained
1 cup (125g) frozen peas
¼ cup (60ml) low-fat cream
2 tablespoons coarsely chopped
   fresh coriander

1 Heat oil in large saucepan; cook onion and garlic, stirring, until onion is soft. Add paste; cook, stirring, until fragrant. Stir in stock and the water, bring to a boil; add pumpkin. Reduce heat; simmer, covered, about 15 minutes or until pumpkin is almost tender.

2 Meanwhile, cook rice in large saucepan of boiling water, uncovered, until tender; drain. Cover to keep warm.

3 Add chickpeas and peas to curry; cook, stirring, until hot. Stir in cream and coriander. Serve curry with rice.

preparation time **10 minutes** cooking time **25 minutes**
serves **4** per serving **12.5g fat; 2631kJ**
tip **Make the curry a day ahead to allow the flavours to develop.**
serving suggestion **Serve with a fresh tomato sambal, pickles or chutney, and pappadums.**

almond, chickpea and pumpkin stew

900g butternut pumpkin, chopped
1 large leek (500g), sliced thinly
2¼ cups (585g) bottled tomato pasta sauce
1 cup (250ml) water
425g can chickpeas, drained, rinsed
1 tablespoon lemon juice
1 tablespoon ground cumin
½ cup (70g) slivered almonds, roasted
¾ cup (200g) yogurt
2 tablespoons finely chopped fresh mint

1 Cook pumpkin and leek in heated oiled large frying pan, stirring, until leek is soft.
2 Stir in sauce, the water, chickpeas, juice and cumin; bring to a boil. Reduce heat; simmer, uncovered, about 20 minutes or until pumpkin is tender, stirring occasionally.
3 Stir in nuts; serve with combined yogurt and mint.

preparation time **10 minutes** cooking time **35 minutes**
serves **4** per serving **15g fat; 1659kJ**

ricotta and spinach lasagne

1kg spinach, trimmed
3 eggs, beaten lightly
2 cups (400g) ricotta cheese
¼ cup (20g) coarsely grated
     parmesan cheese
3 green onions, chopped finely
1½ cups (390g) bottled tomato pasta sauce
12 sheets instant lasagne
1 cup (120g) coarsely grated cheddar cheese

1 Preheat oven to 180°C/160°C fan-forced.
2 Boil, steam or microwave spinach until just wilted; drain. Squeeze excess liquid from spinach; chop roughly. Combine eggs, ricotta, parmesan and onion in large bowl; stir in spinach.
2 Spread half the pasta sauce over base of shallow oiled large baking dish; cover with 3 sheets lasagne, top with a third of the spinach mixture. Cover spinach layer with 3 sheets lasagne; repeat layering with remaining spinach mixture and remaining lasagne sheets. Top lasagne with remaining pasta sauce; sprinkle with cheddar cheese.
3 Cover lasagne with foil; bake 40 minutes.
4 Remove foil; bake about 20 minutes or until browned on top.

preparation time **25 minutes** cooking time **1 hour**
serves **4** per serving **29.1g fat; 2713kJ**

felafel with tangy garlic sauce

We used packaged felafel mix for this recipe, available from Middle-Eastern food shops and many health food stores.

1½ cups felafel mix
⅓ cup (55g) burghul
½ cup finely chopped fresh flat-leaf parsley
1 tablespoon ground coriander
1¼ cups (310ml) water
vegetable oil, for deep-frying
⅓ cup (80ml) water, extra
⅓ cup (80ml) tahini
⅓ cup (80ml) lemon juice
2 cloves garlic, crushed

1 Combine felafel mix, burghul, parsley, coriander and the water in large bowl; refrigerate, covered, about 2 hours or until liquid is absorbed and mixture holds together. [Can be prepared ahead to this point; refrigerate overnight or freeze]
2 Shape level tablespoons of mixture into patties. Heat oil in large frying pan; deep-fry patties, in batches, until browned and cooked through. Drain on absorbent paper.
3 Whisk remaining ingredients in small bowl until smooth; drizzle over felafel. Serve with pitta bread, sliced tomato and lettuce, if you like.

preparation time 20 minutes cooking time 10 minutes
serves 4 per serving 22g fat; 1521kJ

mixed vegetable korma

¼ cup (60ml) korma paste
1 tablespoon black mustard seeds
1.5kg butternut pumpkin, chopped coarsely
⅓ cup (65g) red lentils
2 cups (500ml) vegetable stock
500g cauliflower, chopped coarsely
½ cup (125ml) low-fat cream
200g baby spinach leaves

1 Cook paste and seeds in heated large frying pan until fragrant.
2 Add pumpkin, lentils and stock; bring to a boil. Reduce heat; simmer, covered, 5 minutes. Add cauliflower; simmer, covered, about 10 minutes or until pumpkin is just tender, stirring occasionally.
3 Add cream and spinach; stir until spinach just wilts.

preparation time **5 minutes** cooking time **30 minutes**
serves **4** per serving **17.2g fat; 1607kJ**

eggplant rolls

1 large red capsicum (350g)
1 large yellow capsicum (350g)
2 large eggplants (1kg), sliced thinly
    lengthways
4 medium zucchini (480g), sliced thinly
¼ cup (60ml) olive oil
¼ cup (35g) sun-dried tomatoes in oil,
    drained, chopped finely
400g artichoke hearts, drained,
    chopped finely
125g fetta cheese, crumbled
2 tablespoons olive oil, extra
1 tablespoon balsamic vinegar

1 Preheat oven to 220°C/200°C fan-forced.
2 Quarter capsicums; discard seeds and membranes. Place on oven trays, skin-side up, with eggplant and zucchini slices. Brush vegetables with oil; roast, uncovered, about 5 minutes or until browned. Turn eggplant and zucchini; bake 5 minutes or until softened. Cool.
2 Chop cooled zucchini and capsicum finely; combine in small bowl with the tomato, artichoke and fetta. Divide vegetable mixture equally among eggplant slices; roll carefully, then place seam-side down, in shallow large baking dish. [Can be prepared ahead to this point; refrigerate overnight or freeze]
3 Drizzle half the combined extra oil and vinegar over rolls; bake, covered, about 15 minutes or until hot. Drizzle rolls with remaining combined extra oil and vinegar.

preparation time **25 minutes** cooking time **25 minutes**
serves **4** per serving **32.2g fat; 1828kJ**

baked semolina with tomato and olive sauce

2 cups (500ml) vegetable stock
2 cups (500ml) milk
1 cup (160g) semolina
1 egg, beaten lightly
1 cup (125g) coarsely grated cheddar cheese
1 cup (80g) coarsely grated parmesan cheese
3 cups (780g) bottled tomato and basil
   pasta sauce
⅓ cup (40g) seeded black olives, sliced thinly
2 tablespoons finely chopped fresh oregano
2 teaspoons sugar

1 Bring stock and milk to a boil in large saucepan. Stir in semolina; cook, stirring, about 15 minutes or until mixture thickens. Stir in the egg, half of the cheddar and three-quarters of the parmesan; spread semolina evenly into oiled deep 19cm-square cake pan. Cover; refrigerate 2 hours or until firm. [Can be prepared ahead to this point; refrigerate up to 3 days]

2 Preheat oven to 220°C/200°C fan-forced.

3 Turn semolina onto board; cut in half, then cut each half into 1cm slices. Combine pasta sauce, olive, oregano and sugar in medium bowl; spoon half the tomato sauce mixture into oiled 3 litre (12-cup) ovenproof dish; top with overlapping slices of semolina. Drizzle remaining tomato sauce mixture over semolina; sprinkle with remaining cheeses.

4 Bake, covered, 20 minutes. Remove cover; bake 10 minutes or until browned lightly. Stand 10 minutes before serving.

preparation time **20 minutes (plus standing time)**
cooking time **50 minutes**
serves **4** per serving **26g fat; 2467kJ**

spanish tortilla with spicy tomato sauce

4 medium potatoes (800g)
⅓ cup (80ml) olive oil
5 eggs, beaten lightly
1 medium brown onion (150g),
    chopped finely
2 cloves garlic, crushed
410g can crushed tomatoes
1 teaspoon chilli powder

1   Boil, steam or microwave potatoes until just tender; drain. Slice potatoes thinly.
2   Heat 1 tablespoon of the oil in 24cm frying pan; arrange potato in pan, pour eggs over potato. Cook, tilting pan, over medium heat until omelette is almost set. Drizzle 1 tablespoon of the oil over omelette; place pan under heated grill until top is browned. Stand 5 minutes, turn onto serving platter; cover to keep warm.
3   Heat remaining oil in same pan; cook onion and garlic, stirring, until onion is soft. Add undrained tomatoes and chilli; cook, uncovered, about 5 minutes or until sauce thickens. Serve sauce with omelette.

preparation time **15 minutes (plus standing time)**
cooking time **30 minutes**
serves **4** per serving **25.3g fat; 1775kJ**

cheesy stuffed mushrooms

12 flat mushrooms (960g)
40g butter
1 medium brown onion (150g),
   chopped finely
2 cloves garlic, crushed
½ small red capsicum (100g),
   chopped finely
½ bunch spinach (250g),
   shredded finely
1 tablespoon finely chopped fresh basil
1 teaspoon dried tarragon leaves
150g fetta cheese, crumbled
1½ cups (100g) stale breadcrumbs
tomato sauce
3 teaspoons cornflour
1½ cups (375ml) water
⅓ cup (90g) tomato paste

1 Discard stems from mushrooms. Melt butter in large frying pan; add onion and garlic, cook, stirring, until onion is soft. Add capsicum, spinach, basil and tarragon; cook, stirring, until capsicum is tender. Combine vegetable mixture, cheese and breadcrumbs in large bowl.

2 Preheat oven to 180°C/160°C fan-forced.

3 Make tomato sauce.

4 Place mushrooms on oven tray, top with vegetable mixture. Bake, uncovered, about 10 minutes or until hot. Serve mushrooms with tomato sauce.

tomato sauce Blend cornflour with a little of the water in small saucepan, stir in remaining water and paste. Stir over heat until mixture boils and thickens.

preparation time **20 minutes** cooking time **30 minutes**
serves **4** per serving **19.4g fat; 1711kJ**
tip Spinach seasoning and tomato sauce can be prepared a day ahead.

polenta wedges with ratatouille

3 cups (750ml) vegetable stock
1 cup (250ml) water
1 cup (170g) polenta
½ cup (40g) coarsely grated romano cheese
¼ cup (60ml) olive oil
1 large brown onion (200g), sliced thickly
2 medium red capsicums (400g),
    sliced thinly
3 medium zucchini (360g), sliced
    thinly lengthways
410g can crushed tomatoes
¼ cup (75g) tomato paste
2 tablespoons bottled pesto

1 Oil 22cm-round sandwich cake pan.
2 Bring stock and the water to a boil in large saucepan; add polenta. Reduce heat; simmer, stirring, about 10 minutes or until polenta thickens. Stir in cheese. Press polenta into pan; cover, refrigerate 30 minutes or until set.
3 Heat 1 tablespoon of the oil in large frying pan; cook onion, stirring, until just soft. Add capsicum, zucchini, undrained tomatoes, paste and pesto to pan; bring to a boil. Reduce heat; simmer, uncovered, until vegetables are tender.
4 Meanwhile, turn polenta onto board; cut into 8 wedges. Heat remaining oil in large frying pan; cook polenta wedges, in batches, until browned both sides. Serve polenta wedges with ratatouille.

preparation time **20 minutes** cooking time **25 minutes**
serves **4** per serving **22.7g fat; 1870kJ**

vegetable and red lentil soup

Used since prehistoric times, lentils are an excellent source of protein, fibre and B vitamins. As the Hindu proverb says: "Rice is good, but lentils are my life".

2 tablespoons mild curry paste
410g can crushed tomatoes
3 cups (750ml) chicken stock
1 large carrot (180g), chopped finely
2 trimmed celery stalks (200g),
   chopped finely
1 medium potato (200g), chopped finely
1 large zucchini (150g), chopped finely
¾ cup (150g) red lentils
½ cup (60g) frozen peas
⅓ cup (80ml) light coconut milk
2 tablespoons coarsely chopped
   fresh coriander

1 Cook curry paste in large saucepan, stirring, about 1 minute or until fragrant. Add undrained tomatoes, stock, carrot, celery, potato and zucchini; bring to a boil. Reduce heat; simmer, covered, 5 minutes.

2 Add lentils; return to a boil. Reduce heat; simmer, uncovered, about 10 minutes or until lentils are just tender. Add peas; return to a boil. Reduce heat; simmer, uncovered, until peas are just tender.

3 Remove soup from heat; stir in remaining ingredients.

preparation time **5 minutes** cooking time **25 minutes**
serves **6** per serving **4.4g fat; 696kJ**
tip **A hotter curry paste or some finely chopped chilli can be added to boost the flavour.**

vegetable and tofu stir-fry

Tofu, also known as bean curd, is made from the "milk" of crushed soy beans. Its fairly mild flavour is enhanced by the vegetables and sauce.

250g fresh firm tofu
250g fresh rice noodles
1 tablespoon peanut oil
1 large brown onion (200g), sliced thickly
2 cloves garlic, crushed
1 teaspoon five-spice powder
300g button mushrooms, halved
200g swiss brown mushrooms, halved
¼ cup (60ml) japanese soy sauce
1 cup (250ml) vegetable stock
¼ cup (60ml) water
300g baby bok choy, chopped coarsely
300g choy sum, chopped coarsely
4 green onions, chopped coarsely
2½ cups (200g) bean sprouts

1 Cut tofu into 2cm cubes. Place noodles in large heatproof bowl; cover with boiling water, separate with fork, drain.

2 Heat oil in wok or large frying pan; stir-fry brown onion and garlic until onion is soft. Add five-spice; stir-fry until fragrant. Add mushrooms; stir-fry until just tender.

3 Add combined sauce, stock and the water; bring to a boil. Add buk choy, choy sum and green onion; stir-fry until buk choy just wilts. Add tofu, noodles and sprouts; stir-fry until hot.

preparation time **10 minutes** cooking time **15 minutes**
serves **4** per serving **9.3g fat; 1321kJ**

pasta

gnocchi al quattro formaggi

Four cheeses is one of the most delectable (and among the richest!) of all the Italian classic sauces. Here, we team it with gnocchi, but it also marries well with fettuccine or tagliatelle.

¼ cup (60ml) dry white wine
1 cup (250g) mascarpone cheese
1 cup (120g) coarsely grated fontina cheese
½ cup (40g) coarsely grated
    parmesan cheese
¼ cup (60ml) milk
625g potato gnocchi
75g gorgonzola cheese, crumbled

1 Bring wine to a boil in large saucepan; boil, uncovered, until wine reduces by half. Reduce heat, add mascarpone; stir until mixture is smooth. Add fontina, parmesan and milk; cook, stirring, until cheeses melt and sauce is smooth in consistency.
2 Meanwhile, cook gnocchi in large saucepan of boiling water, uncovered, until gnocchi rise to the surface and are just tender; drain.
3 Add gnocchi and gorgonzola to sauce; toss gently to combine.

preparation time **10 minutes** cooking time **10 minutes**
serves **4** per serving **52.3g fat; 3068kJ**

angel hair frittata

100g angel hair pasta
1 tablespoon vegetable oil
1 small leek (200g), chopped coarsely
2 cloves garlic, crushed
¼ cup (20g) finely grated parmesan cheese
200g fetta cheese, crumbled
60g baby spinach leaves, chopped coarsely
½ cup (120g) sour cream
¼ teaspoon ground nutmeg
6 eggs, beaten lightly

1 Cook pasta in large saucepan of boiling water, uncovered, until just tender; drain.
2 Meanwhile, heat oil in 20cm frying pan; cook leek and garlic, stirring, until leek is soft.
3 Combine pasta and leek mixture in large bowl with cheeses, spinach, sour cream, nutmeg and egg. Pour mixture into same frying pan, cover; cook, over low heat, 10 minutes.
4 Remove cover; place under heated grill about 5 minutes or until frittata sets and top browns lightly. Stand in pan 5 minutes before serving.

preparation time **10 minutes** cooking time **20 minutes**
serves **4** per serving **38.4g fat; 2202kJ**
tip Angel hair pasta, the finest of pastas, produces the best results in this frittata because it lends a smooth-textured consistency.

fresh tomato and caper salsa with penne

375g penne
6 medium tomatoes (900g), seeded,
    chopped finely
1/3 cup (80g) drained capers,
    chopped coarsely
1 medium red onion (170g), chopped finely
12 basil leaves, torn
12 thai basil leaves, torn
1/2 cup (80g) toasted pine nuts
balsamic vinaigrette
2 cloves garlic, crushed
1/3 cup (80ml) balsamic vinegar
2/3 cup (160ml) olive oil

1 Cook pasta in large saucepan of boiling water, uncovered, until tender; drain. Rinse until cold water; drain.
2 Meanwhile, make balsamic vinaigrette.
3 Place pasta in large bowl with remaining ingredients; add balsamic vinaigrette, toss gently to combine.
balsamic vinaigrette Combine ingredients in screw-top jar; shake well.

preparation time **15 minutes** cooking time **10 minutes**
serves **4** per serving **51.7g fat; 2297kJ**

minestrone on the run

1 tablespoon olive oil

1 medium brown onion (150g),
    chopped finely

2 cloves garlic, crushed

1 large carrot (180g), chopped coarsely

3 trimmed celery stalks (300g),
    chopped coarsely

2 medium parsnips (250g), chopped coarsely

2 x 425g cans whole peeled tomatoes

2 tablespoons tomato paste

3 cups (750ml) vegetable stock

1½ cups (375ml) water

180g small macaroni

400g can borlotti beans, drained, rinsed

¼ cup coarsely chopped fresh basil

⅓ cup (25g) finely grated pecorino cheese

1 Heat oil in large saucepan; cook onion and garlic, stirring, until onion is soft. Add carrot, celery and parsnip; cook, stirring, 5 minutes. Add undrained tomatoes, paste, stock and the water; bring to a boil. Cook, uncovered, 5 minutes.

2 Add pasta; boil, uncovered, until pasta is just tender.

3 Add beans; stir over low heat until hot. Stir in basil. Serve minestrone sprinkled with cheese.

preparation time **10 minutes** cooking time **25 minutes**
serves **4** per serving **8.7g fat; 1798kJ**
tip **Drained canned cannellini beans (or even chickpeas)
can be substituted for borlotti beans.**

spaghetti and meatballs

500g pork mince
2 tablespoons coarsely chopped fresh
    flat-leaf parsley
1 clove garlic, crushed
1 egg
1 cup (70g) stale breadcrumbs
1 tablespoon tomato paste
2 tablespoons olive oil
410g can crushed tomatoes
2¼ cups (585g) bottled tomato pasta sauce
375g spaghetti
⅓ cup (25g) finely grated romano cheese

1 Combine pork, parsley, garlic, egg, breadcrumbs and paste in large bowl; roll tablespoons of pork mixture into balls. Heat oil in large saucepan; cook meatballs, in batches, until browned.

2 Place undrained tomatoes and sauce in same pan; bring to a boil. Return meatballs to pan, reduce heat; simmer, uncovered, about 10 minutes or until meatballs are cooked through.

3 Meanwhile, cook pasta in large saucepan of boiling water, uncovered, until just tender; drain. Divide pasta among serving bowls; top with meatballs, sprinkle with cheese.

preparation time **15 minutes** cooking time **20 minutes**
serves **4** per serving **23g fat; 3149kJ**
tips Meatballs can be made and fried a day ahead; keep, covered, in the refrigerator until the sauce is made. To save time when making the recipe on another occasion, double the meatball quantities and freeze half of them after frying. Thaw meatballs overnight in refrigerator before adding to the sauce.

linguine al pesto

2 cups firmly packed fresh basil leaves
2 cloves garlic, peeled, quartered
½ cup (40g) coarsely grated
    parmesan cheese
⅓ cup (50g) roasted pine nuts
½ cup (125ml) olive oil
375g linguine

1 Blend or process basil, garlic, cheese and nuts with a little of the olive oil. When basil mixture is just pureed, gradually pour in remaining oil with motor operating; blend until mixture forms a paste.
2 Meanwhile, cook pasta in large saucepan of boiling water, uncovered, until just tender; drain.
3 Combine pasta in large bowl with pesto.

preparation time **15 minutes** cooking time **12 minutes** serves **4** per serving **41.6g fat; 2617kJ**
tip Pesto freezes well so it will see you through the winter if you make several quantities of this recipe when basil is in season. Freeze in ice-cube trays, covered tightly, or individual snap-lock freezer bags. One cube of frozen pesto can be stirred into homemade minestrone or tomato soup to add a piquant taste.

risoni with spinach and semi-dried tomatoes

30g butter
2 medium brown onions (300g),
   chopped finely
3 cloves garlic, crushed
500g risoni
1 litre (4 cups) chicken stock
½ cup (125ml) dry white wine
1 cup (150g) drained semi-dried
   tomatoes in oil, halved
100g baby spinach leaves
⅓ cup (25g) finely grated parmesan cheese

1 Melt butter in large saucepan; cook onion and garlic, stirring, until onion is soft. Add risoni; stir to coat in butter mixture. Stir in stock and wine; bring to a boil. Reduce heat; simmer, stirring, until liquid is absorbed and risoni is just tender. Stir in tomato, spinach and cheese.

preparation time **5 minutes** cooking time **25 minutes**
serves **4** per serving **12.5g fat; 2777kJ**

pasta caesar salad

200g large pasta shells
2 rindless bacon rashers (130g),
  chopped finely
1 medium cos lettuce, torn
2 hard-boiled eggs, chopped coarsely
2 small avocados (400g), chopped coarsely
½ cup (40g) shaved parmesan cheese
caesar dressing
1 egg
2 cloves garlic, quartered
2 tablespoons lemon juice
1 teaspoon dijon mustard
8 anchovy fillets, drained
¾ cup (180ml) olive oil

1 Cook pasta in large saucepan of boiling water, uncovered, until just tender; drain. Rinse under cold water; drain.
2 Meanwhile, cook bacon in small frying pan, stirring, until crisp; drain on absorbent paper.
3 Make caesar dressing.
4 Place pasta and bacon in large bowl with lettuce, hard-boiled egg and avocado; pour over half of the caesar dressing, toss gently to combine.
5 Divide salad among serving plates; drizzle with remaining dressing, sprinkle with cheese.
caesar dressing Blend or process egg, garlic, juice, mustard and anchovies until smooth; with motor operating, gradually add oil, processing until dressing thickens.

preparation time **15 minutes** cooking time **15 minutes**
serves **4** per serving **68.1g fat; 3611kJ**
tip **Caesar dressing can be prepared a day ahead.**

saganaki prawn pasta

500g medium uncooked prawns
2 teaspoons olive oil
1 small brown onion (100g), chopped finely
2 cloves garlic, crushed
2¼ cups (585g) bottled tomato pasta sauce
1 cup (250ml) vegetable stock
375g small pasta spirals
200g fetta cheese, crumbled
2 tablespoons coarsely chopped
    fresh oregano

1 Shell and devein prawns, leaving tails intact.
2 Heat oil in medium saucepan; cook onion and garlic, stirring, until onion is soft. Add prawns; cook, stirring, until prawns change colour.
3 Add sauce and stock; bring to a boil. Reduce heat; simmer, uncovered, about 2 minutes or until hot.
4 Meanwhile, cook pasta in large saucepan of boiling water, uncovered, until just tender; drain.
5 Place pasta in large bowl with prawn mixture, cheese and oregano; toss gently to combine.

preparation time **10 minutes** cooking time **15 minutes**
serves **4** per serving **15.8g fat; 2495kJ**

spaghetti with herbed ricotta

2 cups (400g) fresh ricotta
3 egg yolks
¾ cup (180ml) milk
⅓ cup coarsely chopped fresh
    flat-leaf parsley
¼ cup coarsely chopped fresh basil
3 green onions, chopped finely
2 cloves garlic, crushed
¼ cup (20g) finely grated parmesan cheese
500g spaghetti

1 Cook pasta in large saucepan of boiling water, uncovered, until just tender; drain.
2 Meanwhile, whisk ricotta, egg yolks and milk in large bowl until smooth; stir in herbs, onion, garlic and parmesan.
3 Add pasta to ricotta mixture; toss gently to combine.

preparation time **10 minutes** cooking time **15 minutes**
serves **4** per serving **21.7g fat; 2863kJ**

rigatoni with brie, walnut and mushroom sauce

1 tablespoon olive oil
1 clove garlic, crushed
200g button mushrooms, halved
½ cup (125ml) dry white wine
2 tablespoons wholegrain mustard
600ml light cream
375g rigatoni
200g brie cheese, chopped coarsely
1 cup (100g) roasted walnuts,
    chopped coarsely
¼ cup coarsely chopped fresh chives

1 Heat oil in large frying pan; cook garlic and mushroom, stirring, until mushrooms are just tender. Add wine, bring to a boil; boil, uncovered, until wine reduces by half.
2 Add mustard and cream to mushroom mixture; cook, stirring, until sauce thickens slightly.
3 Meanwhile, cook pasta in large saucepan of boiling water, uncovered, until just tender; drain.
4 Combine pasta, cheese, nuts, chives and sauce in large bowl.

preparation time **5 minutes** cooking time **20 minutes**
serves **4** per serving **77.7g fat; 4686kJ**

ravioli salad with broccoli and basil

375g spinach and ricotta ravioli
4 rindless bacon rashers (260g),
    chopped coarsely
250g broccoli florets
250g cherry tomatoes, halved
2 tablespoons finely shredded fresh basil
½ cup (125ml) olive oil
¼ cup (60ml) white wine vinegar
2 tablespoons sun-dried tomato pesto

1 Cook pasta in large saucepan of boiling water, uncovered, until just tender; drain. Rinse under cold water; drain.

2 Meanwhile, cook bacon in small frying pan, stirring, until crisp; drain on absorbent paper.

3 Boil, steam or microwave broccoli until just tender, drain. Rinse under cold water; drain.

4 Place pasta, bacon and broccoli in large bowl with tomato, basil and combined remaining ingredients; toss gently to combine.

preparation time **15 minutes** cooking time **15 minutes**
serves **4** per serving **37.9g fat; 2205kJ**
tip **You can use any kind of prepared pesto you prefer in the salad dressing: roasted vegetable is a good alternative.**
serving suggestion **This salad can serve as the main course for a light lunch or late supper, accompanied by a simple green salad and a loaf of fresh bread.**

spaghetti marinara

1 tablespoon olive oil
1 medium brown onion (150g),
    chopped finely
⅓ cup (80ml) dry white wine
⅓ cup (95g) tomato paste
2 x 425g cans whole peeled tomatoes
750g marinara mix
¼ cup coarsely chopped fresh
    flat-leaf parsley
375g spaghetti

1 Heat oil in large frying pan; cook onion, stirring, until soft.

2 Add wine, paste and undrained tomatoes to pan; bring to a boil. Reduce heat; simmer, uncovered, about 10 minutes or until sauce thickens slightly.

3 Add marinara mix; cook, stirring, about 5 minutes or until seafood is cooked through. Stir in parsley.

4 Meanwhile, cook pasta in a large saucepan of boiling water, uncovered, until just tender; drain.

5 Serve pasta topped with marinara sauce.

preparation time **5 minutes** cooking time **15 minutes**
serves **4** per serving **10.7g fat; 1932kJ**

tagliatelle puttanesca

2 teaspoons vegetable oil
1 large brown onion (200g), sliced thickly
3 cloves garlic, crushed
4 fresh small red thai chillies,
    chopped finely
2¼ cups (585g) bottled tomato pasta sauce
¼ cup (40g) drained capers
1 cup (120g) seeded black olives
8 anchovy fillets, drained
½ cup coarsely chopped fresh
    flat-leaf parsley
375g tagliatelle

1   Heat oil in large frying pan; cook onion, garlic and chilli, stirring, until onion is soft. Add sauce, capers, olive and anchovies; bring to a boil. Reduce heat; simmer, uncovered, about 5 minutes or until sauce thickens slightly. Stir in parsley.

2   Meanwhile, cook pasta in large saucepan of boiling water, uncovered, until just tender; drain.

3   Combine pasta and sauce in large bowl.

preparation time **10 minutes** cooking time **20 minutes**
serves **4** per serving **6.6g fat; 2195kJ**

macaroni cheese

250g elbow macaroni
60g butter
⅓ cup (50g) plain flour
3 cups (750ml) milk
2 cups (250g) coarsely grated pizza cheese

1 Cook pasta in large saucepan of boiling water, uncovered, until just tender; drain.
2 Meanwhile, melt butter in medium saucepan; add flour, cook, stirring, about 2 minutes or until mixture thickens and bubbles. Gradually stir in milk; cook, stirring, until sauce boils and thickens.
2 Stir pasta and half of the cheese into sauce; pour mixture into shallow 2-litre (8-cup) baking dish. Sprinkle with remaining cheese; place under hot grill until cheese melts and top browns lightly.

preparation time **5 minutes** cooking time **20 minutes**
serves **4** per serving **34.2g fat; 2846kJ**

russian penne salad

This new take on the classic Russian original is great served with grilled pork fillet or cutlets.

375g penne
2 cups (250g) frozen peas
450g can whole baby beets, drained, chopped coarsely
6 green onions, chopped finely
2 cloves garlic, crushed
2 large dill pickles, chopped finely
¼ cup coarsely chopped fresh flat-leaf parsley
1 cup (240g) sour cream
1 cup (250ml) buttermilk

1 Cook pasta in large saucepan of boiling water, uncovered, until just tender; drain. Rinse under cold water; drain.
2 Meanwhile, boil, steam or microwave peas until just tender; drain.
3 Place pasta and peas in large bowl with beet, onion, garlic, pickle, parsley and combined cream and buttermilk; toss gently to combine.

preparation time **15 minutes** cooking time **10 minutes**
serves **4** per serving **26.6g fat; 2753kJ**

glossary

BEAN SPROUTS also known as bean shoots; tender new growths of assorted beans and seeds germinated for consumption as sprouts.

BORLOTTI BEANS also known as roman beans or pink beans, can be eaten fresh or dried. Interchangeable with pinto beans because of the similarity in appearance – both are pale pink or beige with dark red streaks.

BURGHUL also known as bulghur wheat; hulled steamed wheat kernels that, once dried, are crushed into various-sized grains. Used in Middle Eastern dishes such as felafel, kibbeh and tabbouleh. Burghul is not the same thing as cracked wheat, the untreated whole wheat berry broken during milling into a cereal product of varying degrees of coarseness used in bread making.

BUK CHOY also known as bok choy, pak choi, Chinese white cabbage or Chinese chard; has a fresh, mild mustard taste. Use both stems and leaves, stir-fried or braised. Baby buk choy, also known as pak kat farang or shanghai bok choy, is much smaller and more tender than buk choy.

BUTTERMILK in spite of its name, buttermilk is actually low in fat, varying between 0.6 per cent and 2.0 per cent per 100 ml. Originally the term given to the slightly sour liquid left after butter was churned from cream, today it is intentionally made from no-fat or low-fat milk to which specific bacterial cultures have been added during the manufacturing process.

CAYENNE also known as cayenne pepper; a thin-fleshed, long, extremely hot, dried red chilli, usually purchased ground.

CHEESE

Brie often referred in France as the queen of cheeses; soft-ripened cow-milk cheese with a delicate, creamy texture and a rich, sweet taste that varies from buttery to mushroomy.

Cheddar the most common cow-milk tasty cheese; should be aged, hard and have a pronounced bite.

Fetta Greek in origin; a crumbly textured goat- or sheep-milk cheese having a sharp, salty taste. Ripened and stored in salted whey; particularly good cubed and tossed into salads.

Fontina a smooth, firm Italian cow-milk cheese with a creamy, nutty taste and brown or red rind; an ideal melting or grilling cheese.

Gorgonzola a creamy Italian blue cheese having a mild, sweet taste; good as an accompaniment to fruit or used to flavour sauces (especially pasta).

Haloumi a Greek Cypriot cheese having a semi-firm, spongy texture and very salty yet sweet flavour. Ripened and stored in salted whey; it's best grilled or fried, and holds its shape well on being heated.

Mascarpone an Italian fresh cultured-cream product made in much the same way as yogurt. Whiteish to creamy yellow in colour, with a buttery-rich, luscious texture.

Mozzarella soft, spun-curd cheese; originating in southern Italy where it was traditionally made from water-buffalo milk. Now generally manufactured from cow milk, it is the most popular pizza cheese because of its low melting point and elasticity when heated (used for texture rather than flavour).

Parmesan also known as parmigiano, parmesan is a hard, grainy cow-milk cheese which originated in the Parma region of Italy. The curd for this cheese is salted in brine for a month before being aged for up to 2 years, preferably in humid conditions.

Pecorino the Italian generic name for cheeses made from sheep milk. This family of hard, white to pale-yellow cheeses, traditionally made in the Italian winter and spring when sheep graze on natural pastures, have been matured for 8 to 12 months.

Pizza a commercial blend of varying proportions of processed grated mozzarella, cheddar and parmesan.

Provolone a mild stretched-curd cheese similar to mozzarella when young, becoming hard, spicy and grainy the longer it's aged.

Ricotta a soft, sweet, moist, white cow-milk cheese with a low fat content (about 8.5 per cent) and a slightly grainy texture. The name roughly translates as "cooked again" and refers to ricotta's manufacture from a whey that is itself a by-product of other cheese making.

CHOY SUM also known as pakaukeo or flowering cabbage, a member of the buk choy family; easy to identify with its long stems, light green leaves and yellow flowers. Stems and leaves are both edible, steamed or stir-fried.

COS LETTUCE also known as romaine lettuce; the traditional caesar salad lettuce. Long, with leaves ranging from dark green on the outside to almost white near the core; the leaves have a stiff centre rib that gives a slight cupping effect to the leaf on either side.

COUSCOUS a fine, grain-like cereal product made from semolina; from the countries of North Africa. A semolina flour and water dough is sieved then dehydrated to produce minuscule even-sized pellets of couscous; it is rehydrated by steaming or with the addition of a warm liquid and swells to three or four times its original size; eaten like rice with a tagine, as a side dish or salad ingredient.

CORIANDER also known as cilantro, pak chee or chinese parsley; bright-green-leafed herb having both a pungent aroma and taste.

CORN FLAKE CRUMBS a prepared finely ground mixture used for coating or crumbing food before frying or baking, sold as "crushed corn flakes" in 300g packages in most supermarkets.

CURLY ENDIVE also known as frisée; a prickly-looking, curly-leafed green vegetable having an edible white heart. Fairly bitter in flavour (like chicory, with which it is often confused), it is used mainly in salads.

FENNEL also known as finocchio or anise; a crunchy green vegetable slightly resembling celery that's eaten raw in salads; fried as an accompaniment; or used as an ingredient in pasta sauces, soups and sauce. Also the name given to the dried seeds of the plant which have a stronger licorice flavour.

FRESH FIRM TOFU made by compressing bean curd to remove most of the water. Good used in stir-fries as it can be tossed without disintegrating.

FRESH SMALL RED THAI CHILLI also known as "scuds"; tiny, very hot and bright red in colour.

HORSERADISH CREAM a commercially prepared creamy paste consisting of grated horseradish, vinegar, oil and sugar.

KAFFIR LIME LEAVES also known as bai magrood, look like they are two glossy dark green leaves joined end to end, forming a rounded hourglass shape. Sold fresh, dried or frozen, the dried leaves are less potent so double the number if using them as a substitute for fresh; a strip of fresh lime peel may be substituted for each kaffir lime leaf.

KUMARA the polynesian name of an orange-fleshed sweet potato often confused with yam; good baked, boiled, mashed or fried similarly to other potatoes.

LEEK a member of the onion family, the leek resembles a green onion but is much larger and more subtle in flavour.

LEMON GRASS also known as takrai, serai or serah. A tall, clumping, lemon-smelling and tasting, sharp-edged aromatic tropical grass; the white lower part of the stem is used, finely chopped, in much of the cooking of South East Asia. Can be found, fresh, dried, powdered and frozen, in supermarkets and greengrocers as well as Asian food shops.

LEMON PEPPER SEASONING a commercially made blend of crushed black pepper, lemon, herbs and spices; found on supermarket shelves.

MARSALA a fortified Italian wine produced in the region surrounding the Sicilian city of Marsala; recognisable by its intense amber colour and complex aroma.Often used in cooking, especially in sauces, risottos and desserts.

MESCLUN also known as mixed greens or spring salad mix. A commercial blend of assorted young lettuce and other green leaves, including baby spinach leaves, mizuna and curly endive.

MUSHROOM
Button small, cultivated white mushrooms with a mild flavour. When a recipe in this book calls for an unspecified type of mushroom, use button.
Flat large, flat mushrooms with a rich earthy flavour, ideal for filling and barbecuing. They are sometimes misnamed field mushrooms which are wild mushrooms.
Oyster also known as abalone; grey-white mushrooms shaped like a fan. Prized for their smooth texture and subtle, oyster-like flavour.
Swiss brown also known as roman or cremini. Light to dark brown mushrooms with full-bodied flavour; suited for use in casseroles or being stuffed and baked.

MUSTARD
Dijon also known as french. Pale brown, creamy, distinctively flavoured, fairly mild French mustard.

Wholegrain a French-style coarse-grain mustard made from crushed mustard seeds and dijon-style french mustard. Serve with cold meats and sausages.

NOODLES

Fresh rice also known as ho fun, khao pun, sen yau, pho or kway tiau, depending on the country of manufacture; the most common form of noodle used in Thailand. Can be purchased in strands of various widths or large sheets weighing about 500g which are to be cut into the desired noodle size.

Hokkien also known as stir-fry noodles; fresh wheat noodles resembling thick, yellow-brown spaghetti needing no pre-cooking before use.

Rice stick also known assen lek, ho fun or kway teow; especially popular South East Asian dried rice noodles. They come in different widths (thin used in soups, wide in stir-fries), but all should be soaked in hot water to soften.

OIL

Cooking spray we use a cholesterol-free spray made from canola oil.

Olive made from ripened olives. Extra virgin and virgin are the first and second press, respectively, of the olives and are therefore considered the best; the "extra light" or "light" name on other types refers to taste not fat levels.

Peanut pressed from ground peanuts; the most commonly used oil in Asian cooking because of its high smoke point (capacity to handle high heat without burning).

Sesame made from roasted, crushed, white sesame seeds; a flavouring rather than a cooking medium.

Vegetable any of a number of oils sourced from plant rather than animal fats.

PASTA

Orecchiette small disc-shaped pasta, translates literally as "little ears".

Risoni small rice-shape pasta; very similar to another small pasta, orzo.

Spiral corkscrew-shaped pasta available in various flavours and sizes.

Tagliatelle long, flat strips of durum wheat pasta, slightly narrower and thinner than fettuccine.

PASTE

Green hottest of the traditional thai pastes; particularly good in chicken and vegetable curries, and a great addition to stir-fry and noodle dishes.

Korma a classic north Indian sauce with a rich yet delicate coconut flavour and hints of garlic, ginger and coriander.

Tikka masala in Indian cooking, the word "masala" loosely translates as paste and the word "tikka" means a bite-sized piece of meat, poultry or fish, or sometimes a cutlet. Tikka paste is any maker's choice of spices and oils, mixed into a mild paste, frequently coloured red. Used for marinating or for brushing over meat, seafood or poultry, before or during cooking instead of as an ingredient.

POLENTA also known as cornmeal; a flour-like cereal made of dried corn (maize). Also the name of the dish made from it.

POTATO

Baby new also known as chats; not a separate variety but an early harvest with very thin skin. Good unpeeled steamed, eaten hot or cold in salads.

Coliban round, smooth white skin and flesh; good for baking and mashing.

Desiree oval, smooth and pink-skinned, waxy yellow flesh; good in salads, boiled and roasted.

Idaho also known as russet burbank; russet in colour, fabulous baked

Kipfler small, finger-shaped, nutty flavour; great baked and in salads.

Pontiac large, red skin, deep eyes, white flesh; good grated, boiled and baked.

PROSCIUTTO a kind of unsmoked Italian ham; salted, air-cured and aged, it is usually eaten uncooked. There are many styles of prosciutto, one of the best being Parma ham, from Italy's Emilia Romagna region, traditionally lightly salted, dried then eaten raw.

RICE

Basmati a white, fragrant long-grained rice; the grains fluff up beautifully when cooked. It should be washed several times before cooking.

Jasmine or Thai jasmine, is a long-grained white rice recognised around the world as having a perfumed aromatic quality; moist in texture, it clings together after cooking. Sometimes substituted for basmati rice.

Long-grain elongated grains that remain separate when cooked; this is the most popular steaming rice in Asia.

RICE PAPER SHEETS made from rice flour and water then stamped into rounds; quite brittle and break easily. Dipped briefly in water, they become pliable wrappers for food.

ROCKET also known as arugula, rugula and rucola; peppery green leaf eaten raw in salads or used in cooking. Baby rocket leaves are smaller and less peppery.

SAGE pungent herb with narrow, grey-green leaves; slightly bitter with a slightly musty mint aroma.

SAUCE

Barbecue spicy, tomato-based sauce used to marinate, baste or as an accompaniment.

Fish called naam pla on the label if Thai-made, nuoc naam if Vietnamese; the two are almost identical. Made from pulverised salted fermented fish (most often anchovies); has a pungent smell and strong taste. Available in varying degrees of intensity, so use according to your taste.

Light soy fairly thin in consistency and, while paler than the others, the saltiest tasting; used in dishes in which the natural colour of the ingredients is to be maintained.

Hoisin a thick, sweet and spicy Chinese barbecue sauce made from salted fermented soybeans, onions and garlic; used as a marinade or baste, or to accent stir-fries and barbecued or roasted foods. From Asian food shops and supermarkets.

Japanese soy an all-purpose low-sodium soy sauce made with more wheat content than its Chinese counterparts; fermented in barrels and aged.

Possibly the best table soy and the one to choose if you only want one variety.

Kecap manis dark, thick sweet soy sauce used in most South East Asian cuisines. Depending on the manufacturer, the sauces's sweetness is derived from the addition of either molasses or palm sugar when brewed. Use as a condiment, dipping sauce, ingredient or marinade.

Oyster Asian in origin, this thick, richly flavoured brown sauce is made from oysters and their brine, cooked with salt and soy sauce, and thickened with starches.

Sweet chilli comparatively mild, fairly sticky and runny bottled sauce made from red chillies, sugar, garlic and white vinegar; used in Thai cooking and as a condiment.

Worcestershire thin, dark-brown spicy sauce developed by the British when in India; used as a seasoning for meat, gravies and cocktails, and as a condiment.

Sambal oelek also ulek or olek; Indonesian in origin, this is a salty paste made from ground chillies and vinegar.

SEMOLINA coarsely ground flour milled from durum wheat; the flour used in making gnocchi, pasta and couscous.

SHALLOT also called french shallots, golden shallots or eschalots. Small, elongated, brown-skinned members of the onion family; they grow in tight clusters similar to garlic.

SPATCHCOCK a small chicken (poussin), no more than 6 weeks old, weighing a maximum of

500g. Also, a cooking term to describe splitting a small chicken open, then flattening and grilling.

TARRAGON often called the king of herbs by the French, it is used as the essential flavouring for many of their classic sauces (béarnaise, tartare, etc).

TAHINI sesame seed paste available from Middle Eastern food stores; most often used in hummus and baba ghanoush.

THYME has tiny grey-green leaves that give off a pungent minty, light-lemon aroma.

TURKISH BREAD also known as pide. Sold in long (about 45cm) flat loaves as well as individual rounds; made from wheat flour and sprinkled with black onion seeds.

VINEGAR

Balsamic originally from Modena, Italy, there are now many balsamic vinegars on the market ranging in pungency and quality depending on how, and for how long, they have been aged. Quality can be determined up to a point by price; use the most expensive sparingly.

Brown malt made from fermented malt and beech shavings.

Cider made from fermented apples.

Raspberry made from fresh raspberries steeped in a white wine vinegar.

Sherry natural vinegar aged in oak according to the traditional Spanish system; a mellow wine vinegar named for its colour.

White made from distilled grain alcohol.

Wine (red, white) made from red and white wine, respectively.

conversion guide

MEASURES

One Australian metric measuring cup holds approximately 250ml; one Australian metric tablespoon holds 20ml; one Australian metric teaspoon holds 5ml.

The difference between one country's measuring cups and another's is within a two- or three-teaspoon variance, and will not affect your cooking results. North America, New Zealand and the United Kingdom use a 15ml tablespoon.

All cup and spoon measurements are level. The most accurate way of measuring dry ingredients is to weigh them. When measuring liquids, use a clear glass or plastic jug with the metric markings.

We use large eggs with an average weight of 60g.

DRY MEASURES

METRIC	IMPERIAL
15g	½oz
30g	1oz
60g	2oz
90g	3oz
125g	4oz (¼lb)
155g	5oz
185g	6oz
220g	7oz
250g	8oz (½lb)
280g	9oz
315g	10oz
345g	11oz
375g	12oz (¾lb)
410g	13oz
440g	14oz
470g	15oz
500g	16oz (1lb)
750g	24oz (1½lb)
1kg	32oz (2lb)

LIQUID MEASURES

METRIC	IMPERIAL
30ml	1 fluid oz
60ml	2 fluid oz
100ml	3 fluid oz
125ml	4 fluid oz
150ml	5 fluid oz (¼ pint/1 gill)
190ml	6 fluid oz
250ml	8 fluid oz
300ml	10 fluid oz (½ pint)
500ml	16 fluid oz
600ml	20 fluid oz (1 pint)
1000ml (1 litre)	1¾ pints

LENGTH MEASURES

METRIC	IMPERIAL
3mm	⅛in
6mm	¼in
1cm	½in
2cm	¾in
2.5cm	1in
5cm	2in
6cm	2½in
8cm	3in
10cm	4in
13cm	5in
15cm	6in
18cm	7in
20cm	8in
23cm	9in
25cm	10in
28cm	11in
30cm	12in (1ft)

OVEN TEMPERATURES

These oven temperatures are only a guide for conventional ovens. For fan-forced ovens, check the manufacturer's manual.

	°C (CELSIUS)	°F (FAHRENHEIT)	GAS MARK
Very slow	120	250	½
Slow	150	275-300	1-2
Moderately slow	160	325	3
Moderate	180	350-375	4-5
Moderately hot	200	400	6
Hot	220	425-450	7-8
Very hot	240	475	9

index

ACP Books

General manager Christine Whiston

Test kitchen food director Pamela Clark

Editorial director Susan Tomnay

Creative director Hieu Chi Nguyen

Director of sales Brian Cearnes

Marketing manager Bridget Cody

Business analyst Rebecca Varela

Operations manager David Scotto

International rights enquiries Laura Bamford
lbamford@acpuk.com

ACP Books are published by ACP Magazines
a division of PBL Media Pty Limited

Group publisher, Women's lifestyle Pat Ingram

Director of sales, Women's lifestyle
Lynette Phillips

Commercial manager, Women's lifestyle
Seymour Cohen

Marketing director, Women's lifestyle Matthew
Dominello

Public relations manager, Women's lifestyle
Hannah Deveraux

Creative director, Events, Women's lifestyle
Luke Bonnano

Research Director, Women's lifestyle
Justin Stone

ACP Magazines, Chief Executive officer
Scott Lorson

PBL Media, Chief Executive officer Ian Law

Produced by ACP Books, Sydney.

Published by ACP Books, a division of
ACP Magazines Ltd, 54 Park St, Sydney;
GPO Box 4088, Sydney, NSW 2001.
phone (02) 9282 8618 fax (02) 9267 9438.
acpbooks@acpmagazines.com.au
www.acpbooks.com.au

Printed and bound in China.

Australia Distributed by Network Services,
phone +61 2 9282 8777 fax +61 2 9264 3278
networkweb@networkservicescompany.com.au

United Kingdom Distributed by Australian
Consolidated Press (UK),
phone (01604) 642 200 fax (01604) 642 300
books@acpuk.com

New Zealand Distributed by Netlink Distribution
Company,
phone (9) 366 9966 ask@ndc.co.nz

South Africa Distributed by PSD Promotions,
phone (27 11) 392 6065/6/7 fax (27 11) 392
6079/80
orders@psdprom.co.za

Canada Distributed by Publishers Group Canada
phone (800) 663 5714 fax (800) 565 3770
service@raincoast.com

A catalogue record for this book is available from
the British Library.
ISBN 978-1-903777-40-4
© ACP Magazines Ltd 2008
ABN 18 053 273 546